X.media.publishing

Springer
Berlin
Heidelberg
New York
Hong Kong
London
Milan
Paris
Tokyo

Frank Thissen

Screen Design Manual

Communicating Effectively Through Multimedia

 Springer

Prof. Dr. Frank Thissen
http://www.frank-thissen.de
E-Mail: frank@frank-thissen.de

Translated from the third edition of the German »Kompendium Screen-Design«
(Springer-Verlag 2003, ISBN 3-540-43552-2)
by James G. Rager, Johnson City, Tennessee, USA

ISSN 1612-1449
ISBN 3-540-43923-4 Springer-Verlag Berlin Heidelberg New York

Library of Congress Cataloging-in-Publication-Data applied for
A catalog record for this book is available from the Library of Congress.
Bibliographic information published by Die Deutsche Bibliothek. Die Deutsche Bibliothek lists this publication in the Deutsche Nationalbibliographie; detailed bibliographic
data is available in the Internet at http://dnb.ddb.de

Springer-Verlag Berlin Heidelberg New York,
a member of BertelsmannSpringer Science+Business Media GmbH
http://www.springer.de

© Springer-Verlag Berlin Heidelberg 2004
Printed in Germany

Cover design: KünkelLopka, Heidelberg
Typesetting and layout through the author
Data preparation: medio Technologies AG, Berlin
Printing and Binding: Stürtz, Würzburg
Printed on acid-free paper   33/3142 ud   5 4 3 2 1 0

»Good design means pertinent information.
Good design means content.
Good design means good surfing, exploring, gathering.«

Roger Black (Web Sites That Work. San José, CA 1997, S. 16)

Table of Contents

Brief Descriptions of the Chapters

Chapter 1—Basics
This chapter explains the term Screen Design and describes its elements. The chapter distinguishes the specific features of multimedia products from those of printed media.

Chapter 2—Orientation and Navigation
Multimedia hypertext systems are more like a space than a book. They can only be used effectively if they enable the user to have a clear orientation and simple navigation. This chapter provides methods and examples for facilitating orientation and navigation.

Chapter 3—Information
How should information be prepared so that it can be used appropriately for digital media? How do people read at a monitor? How do you create suitable and understandable texts?

What do you need to keep in mind when using pictures, videos, and animation? This chapter shows how to prepare content that is appropriate for the medium.

Chapter 4—Screen Layout
This chapter deals with designing the screen so that its contents can be perceived as a unit. How should you place the individual elements? What do you need to keep in mind while doing this? How do people perceive visual arrangements? And how can you use the presentation of structures to clarify relationships?

Chapter 5—Interaction
Interaction is an essential element in multimedia systems. It enables the computer to react to the actions of the user. What does a screen designer need to keep in mind when using interactive elements? What are the boundaries of interactivity? Where does it help, where does it hinder?

Chapter 6—Emotion
Emotions and motivation are central driving forces behind human actions. For this reason, a good multimedia product addresses users not only on a cognitive level, but also on an emotional one and applies specific motivational strategies.

Chapter 7—Intercultural Screen Design
This chapter presents the meaning that a culture has for its members. Because culture always also has to do with identity and is very important to people, you should consider cultural characteristics when designing screens. Various features of cultures are presented and illustrated with examples of how pages should be designed for specific cultures.

Chapter 8—Web Accessibility Initiative
This chapter describes the problems that people with visual disabilities have when using the WWW and shows how to design Web pages so that they are accessible.

Chapter 9—Appendix
The appendix provides references to related literature for further reading and an overview of the sources used.

Preface

Every book is superior to a CD-ROM or Web site.

For example, the pleasure of holding a large, illustrated volume in your hands, paging through it, feeling the exquisite paper, perceiving the quality of the photos and the printing, losing yourself in browsing through, reading and paging—these are the qualities of sensual and intellectual perception that only a well-made book can offer.

Books are extremely flexible; you can read them everywhere—on the train, in bed, in the bathtub. You don't need any electrical outlet or other contrivance. Books are more or less inexpensive and form the basis of our culture. Who could imagine that there would ever come a time when there were no more books?

Every CD-ROM or Web site is superior to a book.

Web sites can be very up-to-date. An author types in text at his PC, sends this text per FTP to a server, and the text can be read worldwide immediately.

A multimedia encyclopedia provides pieces of information that are always only a mouse click away from each other. It can present complex structures clearly and enable the user to display details as needed. Simulations, virtual worlds, complex databases, and the combination not only of time-independent media (text, pictures), but also of time-dependent media (sound, video) offer new possibilities that previously could not be implemented in books. Nothing is as flexible as multimedia systems—do we need books in the future?

This comparison makes it clear that there is no »either…or« where old and new media are concerned; rather, we must consider »both…as well as.« Printed media have their strengths and weaknesses—digital media have theirs also. It is worthwhile to use the strengths and reduce the weaknesses in order to combine new and old media sensibly and appropriately.

This book concerns itself with showing how you can use the strengths of digital media. In so doing, the type of presentation and organization of information that is transported with the help of multimedia CD-ROMs and Web sites plays an essential role. This book would like to help creators of multimedia systems to design digital media appropriately and in a manner oriented to the intended target group. It presents backgrounds and contexts, clarifies them with the help of authentic examples, and encourages the further development of the language of digital media.

This book is based on the findings of the psychology of perception and learning, ergonomics, communications theory, imagery research, semiotics, and aesthetics. Examples help to illustrate these findings. Nevertheless, this book cannot be, and does not intend to be, a »cookbook.« It does not intend consciously to postulate any fixed rules, for inflexible rules are the end of all creativity. Of course, the book does indicate guidelines within which a screen designer should move in order to design his products to be user-friendly and of high quality. Nevertheless, we should have the courage to experiment, to try unusual things, and to go against the rules deliberately, provided that we know those rules already.

We find ourselves just at the beginning of the age of digital information and we are just beginning to learn how to deal with the technologies that have entered our lives in recent years. There will still be many experiments, standards will crystallize, and »gurus« will step onto the stage and then disappear again. The speed with which all this happens before our eyes is breath-taking and fascinating. Where will the journey lead?

This book, now being published in its third German edition, is appearing simultaneously in English language for the first time. Over the years it has grown, has become more extensive, and now, in addition to numerous updates, it contains new chapters on the topic of »Barrier-Free Web Pages« and »Intercultural Screen Design.« The chapter that formerly was called »Motivation« was renamed very consciously to »Emotion« and refers to metacommunicational factors that will continue to gain importance.

I hope that the readers of this book will be inspired to advance the language of digital and interactive media.

I would be very happy to receive letters from readers, including opinions and suggestions.

Frank Thissen
frank@frank-thissen.de

Foreword

by Frieder Nake

We are surrounded by media. Even more: we are submerged in media. We exist in and by media. And we do so increasingly. The digital code in its ubiquity transforms our being and, therefore, transforms ourselves. We hardly recognize it.

Take money as an example! An example of peculiar interest, since money itself is a medium of dominant importance. But it is a commodity at the same time. You have to possess it in order to be able to sustain your life. You do, in fact, possess some of it as long as you are employed and thereby are allowed to work.

Now it occurs that people are prepared to wait in line in order to ask an automaton to kindly supply at least a small amount of their own money. People are willing to identify themselves to the automaton by an elaborate procedure, and thus have the machine mercifully deliver some of the money they own. For the machine, we are nothing but signs. We are willing to produce a set of signals that we hope the machine will interpret as: yes, you are a good person, and you are, indeed, entitled to withdraw some of your money. The money, in turn, is nothing but a sign of work we have performed before, and because of that it may seem odd that

we must undergo, in current times, such a series of semiotic procedures before we are allowed to actually make use of what is our own.

In various other ways, we are nothing but signs to machines and institutions that represent the social fabric to us. The day does not seem to be too far away when we can no longer get into a building without an automatic procedure checking up on us.

We have come to face up to our roles as only signs. »Only signs?« A century ago, Ferdinand de Saussure maintained that I am the individual I think I am, only because language is providing the word »I.« I am able to generate myself as an individual only through that word or similar ones, or delimiting words—but through signs in any case.

Long before constructivism, semioticians have indicated the potential of sign systems to establish reality. We cannot but think through signs, Peirce was convinced. All my thinking takes place by agglomerating and arranging sign complexes around me. The time order is not one of first thinking and then mapping thoughts into appropriate words. Rather, I produce my thought in and with my words. My thought is in my sign. Thought does not exist without, or outside of sign.

The theme of signs is the theme of media. Signs, media, digital media, signs in digital code: they have become the subject matter of a plethora of printed publications. Books abound on screen design or similar titles like Web, interaction, interface, multimedia, hypermedia design. It may sound absurd, but the more diversified the media map becomes, the more books appear.

The most basic and trivial, yet important, facts about those book media remain constant. They come in rectangular shape, consist of a pile of paper sheets that are strongly bound together on the left. They are easy to turn. On the top front, they carry a title. The conclusion is found on the bottom or back pages. Each page is organized, more or less, from top left to bottom right. Even if it is here that differences start, we find our way and keep a general orientation.

The book has become the physical component of an intricate sign system. Important aspects of modern social construction show up in the book medium. They do more than just show up: they exist and develop through the book.

There are thousands of books. There are also thousands of motion pictures. Each one is different from all the others, although motion pictures, too, share some technical aspects. These are so trivial that we hardly take notice of them. We observe them only when they are ignored. Movies are signs, too, as complex as, or more complex than, books.

There are phone calls, too, more signs, and media. We are surrounded by media.

But perhaps the number of books, movies, and phone calls together has already been surpassed by the number of screen pages stored on servers. If this is not the case yet, it soon will be. New signs, sign systems, and codes are created. New universes of signs, new media realities.

In order to function as a sign, a sign has to adhere to some convention. By using one thing instead of another, by distributing it and interpreting it, we create the sign as a sign. Signs are always made, never found, and they are made by humans. Even if we accept the idea that animals use signs, their sign use is of a different kind. A proto-use.

Something becomes a sign by being used as a sign, i.e., by being turned into something more than itself, by pointing at another, or standing for another.

The sign presents itself and re-presents another. Only by present-ing itself can one sign represent another. In representing some other object, the sign designates. But its designating function raises two more functions that immediately become more important: design and interpretation. In fact, a sign emerges by a dialectical process and complex activity between shap-ing some matter, following some intent, and discovering some mean-ing.

The conventions pertaining to the book medium, and rendering the book as part of a semiotic universe, make using a book an easy affair. In a sense, they are arbitrary, and could have developed differently. But once established, we cannot change them voluntarily. As prag-matic people, we don't even want to change them.

In this case as in many others, we are born into universes of signs. As far as human history goes, uni-verses of signs have always been with us, we never had an absolute choice of the whole. Our individual and social choice is only in detail. We tell ourselves a lie—artists that some of us may be—when we claim the opposite. Exactly because

of the pre-existing semiotic environ-ment, I am »I« only through media.

And yet! It does happen that new sign universes are created and new conventions crop up. We know that. We take part in the weaving of it. We should, however, keep some modesty: beyond pri-vate spheres, partially new semiotic universes are occasionally created. For the medium is the message, still. In this brilliant phrase, Marshall McLuhan told us that a new me-dium doesn't, at its outset, express anything different from the old media except for its form, which therefore becomes the essence of the message. This annoying tension gradually leads up to new conven-tions as the medium discovers its peculiarities.

Never before, to mention an ex-ample, has typographic knowledge and awareness been distributed as broadly as today because of every-one's ability to use desktop pub-lishing—even if such typographic sensitivity appears as the aesthetic horrors of DTP.

Is it not a marvel that we may hold in our hands an old medium like the book from which we read passages in generous layout, subtly selected, sharply commented on, luxuriously illustrated, in perma-nently changing design, yet satisfying expectations well enough, consistent in overall design but differently emphasizing detail, ergo with a feeling for style, and presenting lots of data, opinion, insight, and perspective?

Is it not still a wonderful feeling to touch heavy glazed paper, to slide it through the fingers, to turn it, to breathe the smell of print colors, to experience the hard cover, to revel in the brilliance of colors, to get an inkling of a deep insight in the weightless readiness of the word, to get close to the new medium, the screen, via the old book medium along all those paths? Supposedly and hopefully all this approximation happens by design. It happens here! You should turn to Frank Thissen's book if you want to design screens.

Here you meet one man who designs pages of a book that obviously deal with screens. They almost appear as screens in their short sentences, in abstaining from elaborate arguments, in their pictures, in their diversity, in their white space. Typography is the art of shaping white space. Screen design is the art of shaping light—light that never comes to rest but always stays in motion.

Style instead of truth, says Lambert Wiesing in his theory of pure visibility. A handbook is for our hands to take and turn and use. It tells us how to do it. Frank Thissen's book tells you how to do it if you want to. It presents orientation, not law. There is no general truth. Logic is hidden in aesthetics. The aesthetics of screens convinces us to the extent that their logic remains unnoticed. If computer science advice on the design of interfaces is often heavy-handed and coarse, here we find design floating silently and lightly.

When we take Frank Thissen's book in one hand, a glass of red wine in the other, relax and think about what we see on his pages, then we get an increasingly clear idea of where screen design may lead. It may not lead directly to *Gesamtkunstwerk*, even though some would have us believe so. But it is beautifully turned over: from book to screen.

Frieder Nake is a professor for interactive computer graphics at the University of Bremen, Germany. He has contributed to the early development of computer art. His current interest is digital media and aesthetics.

1 Basics

This chapter explains the term Screen Design and describes its elements. The chapter distinguishes the specific features of multimedia products from those of printed media.

1.1 Tasks of Screen Design

»The design is the domain in which the interaction between user and product is structured in order to make effective actions possible.« Gui Bonsiepe

The **term design** is frequently used exclusively in the sense that it is associated with the beautification of products. According to this view, the task of screen design would be merely to lend an aesthetically pleasing appearance to multimedia products.

This book uses an expanded concept of design that interprets screen design primarily as **interface design**. The interface is the connecting link between a tool and the person who is using this tool to do something. The interface helps to operate the tool. An example should clarify this concept: at the left, you see an illustration of a tea bag. In this example, the actual interface of the tea bag is the small green tag. It accomplishes two tasks: on the one hand, it indicates the type of tea; on the other hand—and this is much more important—it facilitates the use of the bag considerably. Have you ever tried to fish a tagless tea bag out of hot water? Then you know how important the tag is. The tag has no effect on the quality of the tea, but it helps considerably in using the tea bag.

The design theoretician Gui Bonsiepe uses his **ontological design diagram** to describe the modern concept of design, which comprehends the interface as the central category of design. This diagram is made up of the following three elements:

- The user
- The task to be handled
- The tool that is required to handle the task

These three areas are connected to each other by the interface. The »interface is the central area to which the designer directs his attention. The design of the interface arranges the procedural space of the person who is using the products. The interface reveals the tool-like characteristics of objects and the informational content of data. The interface turns objects into products. The interface turns data into understandable information.« (Bonsiepe 1996, 20)

The data of a multimedia information system in and of themselves initially have no practical purpose. Only when specific prerequisites have been fulfilled can data become information for the user, be linked to the pervious knowledge of the user, and expand his knowledge:

- The user must be able to recognize and evaluate the relevance of the data for himself.
- The user must be able to relate the data to his previous knowledge.
- The data must be edited in such a way that the user can perceive them, assimilate them, and process them.
- The data must be structured in some sort of form. The user must be able to trace this structure, that is, understand it intuitively.
- The system that provides the data (for example, a digital information system) must react in an appropriate manner to the actions of the user—that is, according to his expectations.

According to this scheme, **screen design** takes on an essential, a central significance. Only when the data can be used effectively do they obtain a value for the user. This is

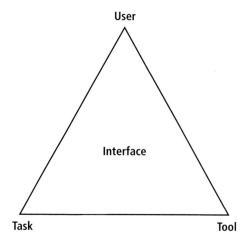

true both for information systems and for tutorials or advertising products. A solid screen design without relevant, useful data is superfluous game playing. Data without an effective screen design have no value for the user because he cannot access them appropriately and therefore it is much harder to use the data.

Both elements—data and interface—must complement each other; they achieve a value for the user only in their combination.

19

1.2 Elements of Screen Design

Effective screen design is distinguished by the functional and aesthetic-harmonic interplay of various elements. The elements introduced here are not always present in their pure function. There are also elements that serve more than one function, as is frequently the case with those elements that are used for both orientation and navigation.

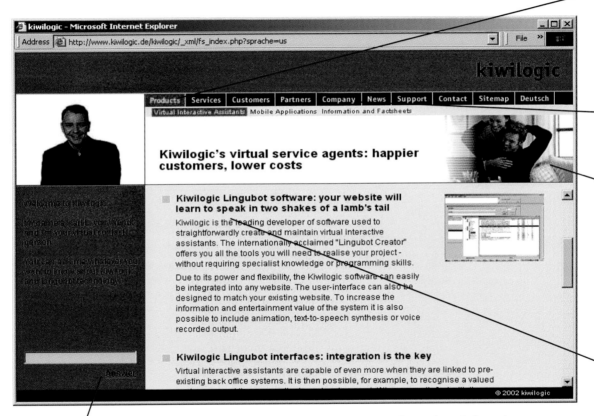

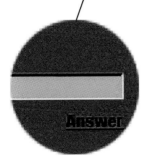

Interaction elements
cause the computer to react to the activities of the user. In this case, a virtual advisor answers the entries of the user.

Screen layout elements
organize the structure of a screen page, relate the contents to each other, and are responsible for a harmonious overall picture. In this example, it is not only the division of the screen contents into various areas, but also the color design.

Orientation elements
allow the user to find his way in hypertext. Using these elements, the user can detect where he is.

Navigation elements
help the user to move around in a multimedia space and to »jump« selectively to specific areas. In the example, the main areas of the site are listed.

Emotion elements
appeal to the feelings of the user; they make him curious and invite him to continue to work with the system.

Content elements
are the edited data, that is, the information, in the form of text, pictures, sounds, videos, or animation.

1.3 More Space Than Book

»… entering a space without any linear limitations or restrictions«
Michael Joyce

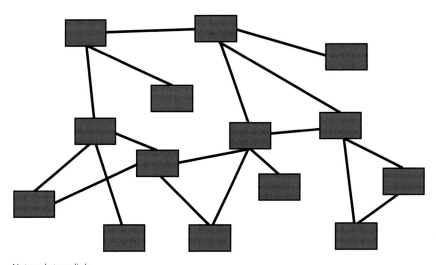

Network-type link

Multimedia is more than just the combination of various media such as text, sound, pictures, video, and animation. Multimedia is a new form of presentation and representation of information with the help of a computer. In this form, the information is indeed coded in various media; what is actually new is the fact that a multimedia system presents its information in small units that are linked to each other in a variety of ways. Documents and links form what is called hypertext.

The basic elements of **hypertext** are nodes, edges, and anchors.

- A **node** is an autonomous, isolated unit that presents specific information with the help of various media.
- An **edge** (hyperlink) connects two units of information (the nodes) to each other. Nodes can have more than one edge.
- **Anchors** are the highlighted points of a node that mark the connection to another node and from which an edge originates.

Complex hypertext systems have a large number of nodes, edges and, anchors. The type of networking of the information unit can be more or less complex and varied.

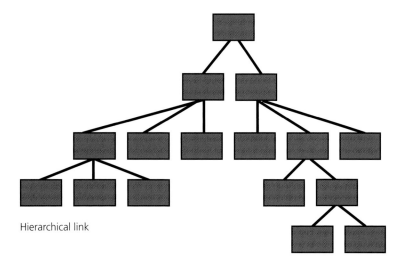

Hierarchical link

Along this network, a user can open up a topic associatively, following his interests, by clicking on the anchors that interest him and in so doing trigger new anchors. Of course, this situation assumes that the author has generated the hypertext in such a manner that it includes the interests and associations of the target audience.

The occasional assertion that, in contrast to hypertext, a printed information medium, such as a book, presents information linearly certainly is not entirely justified. We seldom read even books linearly, from the first page to the last—except for fictional literature; instead, we skip around, follow references and footnotes, or select specific individual chapters. An encyclopedia provides an extreme example. Nevertheless, a book has a certain sequence determined by the author in which it presents information. This sequence has been chosen consciously and reflects the decisions of the author as to the sequence of perception of information that he considers logical. This book that you are reading initially explains the elements of screen design in an overview before presenting them in individual detail in later chapters.

Linear link

In hypertext, there is not a prescribed **sequence**; rather, there are different possibilities for the user to discover the information. Hypertext is made up of networks whose use is determined to a great extent by the particular user and, because of this, these networks can be quite varied. The combination of information units (nodes) that the user makes based on previous knowledge, interests, or curiosity creates quite varied meanings and associations in the user's perception.

»*The **basic idea of hypertext** is that informal units, in which text, graphics, or audio visual aids represent objects and procedures of the relevant section of the world, can be manipulated flexibly by means of links. Manipulation here means primarily that the user can easily place the hypertext units into new contexts that create themselves in that they pursue possible links that appear suitable to them. In this process, the units themselves generally remain unchanged. In the future,* *this idea of manipulation will (have to) be expanded greatly through dialogic principle. Based on this principle, the system can, in and of itself, intervene actively in the dialog with suggestions in order to reduce the complexity that confronts users in working with large volumes of hypertext. If too much is offered and the consequences of choice become too complicated, creativity can easily turn into chaos. Here, hypertext must provide techniques to support mechanically the human information-processing capability, which is limited in a certain respect. Manipulation and cooperative dialog are therefore essential principles of hypertext.*« (Kuhlen 1991, 13)

Not only the node documents, but also the edges are significant. They make it possible to represent logical or argumentative associations by means of linking units of information.

These characteristics can be aptly described by the term **hyperspace**. A hypertext system represents a

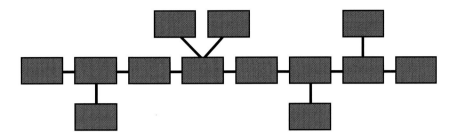

Linear link with branches

space of meaning that the user can open up in various ways.

For the author of multimedia products, this means that he is not the author of a book; rather, he is an **information architect**. His task is to provide various paths through the hyperspace information system and to prepare the individual areas (units of information) and the information that belongs to them. This preparation must enable different users, who have different previous knowledge, expectations, and ways of doing things, to orient themselves and quickly find what they want. For this reason, the information architect should offer orientation aids and indicate navigation paths that put the individual areas into the proper light and make it possible to open up a particular depth of information. In addition, the architect should design the space in an appealing manner and should invite the visitor to visit, awaken his interest, support and motivate him.

1.4 History of Hypertext

The idea of putting information into modules and relating these modules to each other is not new. It goes back to the late 18th century, when the natural sciences were becoming more and more dominant and the age of the enlightenment appeared with the demand that the old shackles of immaturity be removed and that knowledge be made available to all people. What for a long time could only be implemented in a very limited way has become possible today through the World Wide Web. However, standards and quality control are still lacking and the Net presently looks more like a wild shrub as opposed to a structured weave.

In 1751, the French *Encyclopédie, ou dictionnaire raisonné des sciences, des arts et des métiers* (**Encyclopedia**, or Systematic Dictionary of the Sciences, the Arts, and Commerce) appeared, published by Denis Diderot and Jean Le Rond d'Alembert in collaboration with Charles de Secondat Montesquieu, Voltaire, and Jean-Jacques Rousseau. The work appeared with the claim of presenting the current knowledge of the time and clarifying the relationship of the sciences to each other by means of a complex reference system. The authors noted textual relationships to other articles by means of symbolic markings in front of the terms that are explained in more detail in another article.

Up until the year 1772, 28 volumes appeared with a total of 60,000 articles.

ENCYCLOPÉDIE,
OU
DICTIONNAIRE RAISONNÉ
DES SCIENCES,
DES ARTS ET DES MÉTIERS,
PAR UNE SOCIÉTÉ DE GENS DE LETTRES.

Mis en ordre & publié par M. *DIDEROT*, de l'Académie Royale des Sciences & des Belles-Lettres de Prusse ; & quant à la PARTIE MATHÉMATIQUE, par M. *D'ALEMBERT*, de l'Académie Royale des Sciences de Paris , de celle de Prusse , & de la Société Royale de Londres.

Tantùm series juncturaque pollet,
Tantùm de medio sumptis accedit honoris ! HORAT.

TOME PREMIER.

A PARIS,

Chez { BRIASSON, rue Saint Jacques , à la Science.
DAVID l'aîné , rue Saint Jacques , à la Plume d'or.
LE BRETON, Imprimeur ordinaire du Roy, rue de la Harpe.
DURAND, rue Saint Jacques , à Saint Landry, & au Griffon.

M. DCC. LI.
AVEC APPROBATION ET PRIVILEGE DU ROY.

1751

In an article entitled *As We My Think*, **Vannevar Bush**, advisor to President Roosevelt and co-inventor of the analog computer, proposed a machine by the name of MEMEX that was intended to make it possible to store huge amounts of information in the form of notes and to access this information associatively. The users were supposed to have the capability of marking a few connections between passages of text that appeared to them to be contextually related.

»*Consider a future device for individual use, which is a sort of mechanized private file and library. It needs a name, and, to coin one at random, memex will do. A memex is a device in which an individual stores all his books, records, and communications, and which is mechanized so that it may be consulted with exceeding speed and flexibility. It is an enlarged intimate supplement to his memory.*« Vannevar Bush

»*Wholly new forms of encyclopedias will appear, ready made with a mesh of associative trails running through them, ready to be dropped into the memex and there amplified. The lawyer has at his touch the associated opinions and decisions of his whole experience, and of the experience of friends and authorities. The patent attorney has on call the millions of issued patents, with familiar trails to every point of his client's interest. The physician, puzzled by a patient's reactions, strikes the trail established in studying an earlier similar case, and runs rapidly through analogous case histories, with side references to the classics for the pertinent anatomy and histology. The chemist, struggling with the synthesis of an organic compound, has all the chemical literature before him in his laboratory, with trails following the analogies of compounds, and side trails to their physical and chemical behavior. The historian, with a vast chronological account of a people, parallels it with a skip trail which stops only on the salient items, and can follow at any time contemporary trails which lead him all over civilization at a particular epoch. There is a new profession of trail blazers, those who find delight in the task of establishing useful trails through the enormous mass of the common record. The inheritance from the master becomes, not only his additions to the world's record, but for his disciples the entire scaffolding by which they were erected.*« Vannevar Bush, As We May Think

In 1962, **Douglas Engelbart** started his project Augment
at the Stanford Research Institute. As part of this project, the **NLS (oN-Line System)** was developed, an initial
hypertext that consisted of documents, reports, notes,
and letters that were linked to each other and were
stored in a commonly accessible »diary.« At a conference in 1968, the system was presented with over
100,000 entries.

Ted Nelson designed his hypertext system
Xanadu® and used the words »hypertext«
and »hypermedia« for the first time. Xana-
du® was intended to be a universal archive
for all sorts of information, a worldwide
network of text, graphics, and pictures. The
system was never implemented in the form
in which it was originally intended. However,
parts of the system have been marketed by
the Xanadu Operating Company since 1990.
Presently, Nelson is working on the New
Xanadu® Structure for the Web
xanadu.com/nxu and his Cosmicbook
xanadu.com/cosmicbook.

1962   1965

The **Architecture Machine Group** of MIT presented their **Aspen Movie Map**, the first hypermedia videodisc. It contains photographs of all the streets in the city of Aspen, Colorado, USA. These pictures were taken from trucks with four cameras aimed at a 90^0 angle in four different directions. New pictures were taken every three meters. The relevant pictures are linked to each other on the disc. The user can »click his way through« the streets of the city and have the feeling that he is driving through the city.

Available since 1983 is the commercial **Knowledge Management System (KMS)**, a system that manages a large variety of hypertext nodes under UNIX on local area networks. It is a further development of the ZOG research system that was developed at the Carnegie-Mellon University starting in 1972.

The structure of KMS is hierarchical, and you can expand it any way you want with the help of a scripting language. The speed with which the called nodes are displayed is impressive.

Hyperties is a hypertext system developed by **Ben Shneiderman** in 1983 at the University of Maryland. Since 1987, the system has been marketed and developed further by Cognetics Corporation. The system gives a very Spartan impression in that it has been purposely designed to be simple and is geared toward easy operation. Users are advised to set up only a few links, and there are only unidirectional links.

1978   1983

The **HyperCard** program by **Bill Atkinson** was very popular and widely disseminated; between 1987 and 1992, it was included with every Macintosh computer free of charge. It replaced the program Guide that appeared in 1986. HyperCard is based on the index card metaphor, that is, virtual cards are filled out and placed in a stack. They contain text, pictures, video, sound, and links to other cards. Although a beginner could operate it intuitively, it offered the expert many capabilities by means of its programming language HyperTalk.

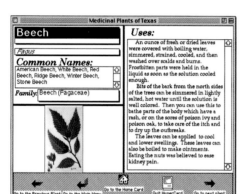

In 1987, the **Association for Computing Machinery (ACM)** held an **initial conference** on the topic of Hypertext at the University of North Carolina. The interest was so great that not all registrants could be accepted and the conference was overcrowded.

1987

The British information scientist **Tim Berners-Lee** published his *Proposal* at the European Center for Nuclear Research CERN in Switzerland and in so doing founded the **World Wide Web**. Originally, his intention was to promote the communication of the CERN scientists and to overcome limitations that were caused by different computer and operating systems as well as different data formats. Through the document text markup language HTML and the development of powerful browsers, the WWW has experienced a rapid dissemination since the beginning of the 1990s. Thousands of Web pages are added daily and expand the weave of (valuable and useless) information. The Web is hypertext—but hypertext that proliferates chaotically and is presently still relatively confusing, unstructured, and hardly user-friendly.

31

1989

1.5 User Oriented Design

»If you don't know who you're talking to, how the heck do you know what to say?«
Nick Usborne

The **basis of every screen design** is the question as to what the user of the product wants to do with the product and how he will do it. Clarification of this question makes the difference between success and failure.

Even the best content and assertions, the most innovative game, and the most effective tutorial will be well received only if they speak the language of the user; that is, if they appeal to him emotionally, they consider his previous knowledge and experience, and they offer him something useful or interesting. The »language« that the user understands depends on many factors: life experiences, cultural surroundings, gender, age, and occupation. A game that a fifteen-year-old school child finds fascinating seems silly to a fifty-year-old engineer. A reference work on anatomy on CD can be extremely helpful to a medical student and still be just about useless to a lawyer. A Web site of the British comedy group Monty Python meets with enthusiasm from those who like British humor; for people who do not like this type of humor, the site is incomprehensible and objectionable. It is impossible for you to appeal to everyone at the same time; instead, you must decide specifically for whom your product is to be used, whose language you want to speak, and with whom you will be communicating. Only then can you decide what the goal of your multimedia product should be, what it should contain, and how you will structure and design it. The more precisely and concretely you view your **target group** and can put yourself in their place, the more successful you will be in reaching them. For this reason it is also advisable to include members of this target group very early in your planning and to test the first prototypes with them.

It is worthwhile to pay close attention to the target group and to expend time and energy to focus on the audience precisely.

The following material presents an extremely effective method for developing a user-oriented screen design.

Personas: a real world example

If an auto manufacturer tried to build a car that pleased every possible driver...

...it might look like this. Instead of pleasing everyone, the vehicle pleases no one.

What if instead the manufacturer chose three specific drivers who were representative of larger groups of similar drivers, and tried to please each of them?

Marge, *mother of three*

Marge wants safety and room for many passengers. A minivan meets her needs.

Jim, *construction worker*

Jim wants cargo space and the ability to carry heavy loads. A pickup meets his needs.

Alesandro, *software engineer*

Alesandro wants sporty looks and speed. A two-door sports car meets his needs.

What's the point of designing for a specific target group? Why make the effort to define specific target groups? After all, our Web material is supposed to address all interested parties. So we have to construct material for everyone and not be too specific, otherwise we exclude users.

These objections are justified because Web pages can be called up worldwide without limitation. The only problem is, that when you offer »something for everyone,« ultimately you don't reach anyone or address anyone appropriately.

The American ergonomics specialist and expert in interaction design, Alan Cooper, uses an automobile as an example to demonstrate very clearly the problem with trying to offer a product that is suitable for everyone.

Different people need different cars because they want to achieve very different goals with their cars. While safety and comfort are especially important to Marge as a mother, Jim needs lots of room, and Alesandro would like to impress his girlfriend. One car for everyone wouldn't please any one of these people and they definitely wouldn't buy it.

33

1.6 Personas

»**The Elastic User**
Although satifying the user is our goal, the term 'user' causes trouble. Its imprecision makes it unusable, like trying to remove someone's appendix with a chainsaw. We need a more precise design tool.

Whenever I hear the phrase 'the user', it sounds to me like 'the elastic user'. The elastic user must bend and stretch and adapt to the needs of the moment. However, our goal is to design software that will bend and stretch and adapt to the user's needs. [...] In our design process, we never refer to the 'user'. Instead, we refer to a very special individual: a persona.«
Alan Cooper

In order to solve the problem of non-specific target groups, I would like to introduce a method here that Alan Cooper developed for defining and designing user interfaces: the so-called **personas concept**. This methodology is very effective and can be applied extremely well to material that appears on the Web.

The point of departure here is a precise description of the users and their goals. Cooper calls this **goal-directed design**.

To achieve this, you define so-called personas. A persona is not a real person, but the archetype of a user; the persona is a cliché, the generalization of a specific user group.

Personas are defined by the things that they want to achieve (their goals). In the definition, they become very lifelike and graphic; they are a great help to the developer in putting himself in the position of the potential user and in communicating about the user in the development team. In this respect, we are no longer talking about the target group of the »new male customers between 35 and 50,« but about the persona Michael Miller and his goals, expectations, and traits.

To ensure that the persona appears vividly to all the participants in the project, it is important to give the persona a name and a »face.« Describe the concrete goals of the persona and typical scenarios in which the persona will use what you have to offer.

In this manner, you can design material very effectively that meets very accurately the requirements of this persona—and in so doing, those of the real user.

Overview: the Procedure for Defining Personas

1. In a brainstorming session with the development team (without any evaluation), collect all relevant personas initially.
   Alan Cooper warns against using real people as personas. Also, personas should not be used more than once. Each project should develop its own personas.

2. The next step is to select from the total of all defined personas the so-called primary personas. These are the personas that will help us to design our Web material. It is better to concentrate on a few personas (no more than four) than to try to accommodate too many. You will find that among the personas whom you have defined, there will be those who have similar goals or who are very similar to other personas. Sometimes personas that are very similar to each other can be combined into a new persona.

3. For each of the personas that you select, create a »dossier« or profile, in which »personal data« are outlined. Give each persona a »face« (picture) and a name.

4. In addition, write in the dossier the most important goals that the persona has in relation to the use of your product.

5. Put yourself in the place of each of these personas; put on their »glasses« and try approaching your product (for example, the Web site) with this view of things. As the persona, ask questions about the product.

6. Structure the questions and define the answers to them.

7. Determine how you want to address the persona, that is, which form of address is appropriate. In so doing, keep in mind the emotional components, too.

8. Only now should you begin to think about the informational material to be used in your presentation to the persona and about the structure of your site and the general layout.

»Personas are not real people, but they represent them throughout the design process. They are hypothetical archetypes of actual users.« Alan Cooper

A Real-Life Example

As an example of the procedure to develop a Web site with the help of personas, I would like to use the Web material of the Information Design course of study at our College of Media (in Stuttgart, Germany). This course of study—which so far is the only one of its kind in Germany—deals with the contextual and formal preparation of information for the most varied media.

In an initial brainstorming session, a group of students in this course of study defined all possible personas for the Web material. Included were the following personas:

- A schoolgirl who is looking for a course of study that is interesting and full of promise for the future
- The personnel manager of a company who is looking for trainees for the Corporate Communications department
- An employee of an advertising agency who is looking for work-study trainees
- A student in the Information Design course of study who is looking for information on the current semester
- A communications designer who would like to further his education in the area of information design
- A professor in a similar course of study who is looking for a professional exchange with colleagues
- A candidate who would like to apply for a newly posted position as professor in the course of study at the college and now is looking for information for the application
- A journalist who is doing research on the field of information design in order to write an article on the subject of information design.

On the basis of this list, the various personas were compared to each other and divided into groups. Then, in long discussions, the group decided to limit itself to four personas for the Web material:

- The personnel manager who had a lot in common with the employee from the advertising agency
- The communications designer who would like to further his education in the area of information design
- The student in the course of study
- The interested schoolgirl.

In order to further clarify the procedure, I will limit myself in the following discussion to the *schoolgirl* persona. Of course, this procedure must be followed for all relevant personas.

On the opposite page you see the dossier of the persona Maria Schneider.

Maria represents the users who at the end of their high school studies are looking for a suitable college or university. In order to allow her to become especially concrete and »lifelike,« her dossier contains a few personal data that clarify her living situation.

Maria's most important goals are listed below. Here it is important not to confuse the goals of the personas with the tasks of the personas. By carrying out tasks, we want to achieve certain goals. For example, no one wants to take a language course; instead, people want to learn a foreign language. Attending a language course is the task which helps to achieve the goal of language competency.

Maria's goals are to be able to have an interesting profession that is associated with social prestige and an adequate salary. When she visits our Web site, she will want to know if she can indeed achieve these goals with the course of study offered. More is involved here than just a few facts. The point is to decide whether and how she can achieve her personal goals.

Maria Schneider

- Age: 18
- Has a sister who is three years younger
- Is a senior at an academic high school in Chicago
- Special subjects: English and art
- Still lives at home
- Has a boyfriend
- Likes to surf the WWW
- Has a positive attitude toward computers, but does not see herself as an expert or computer freak
- Uses her cell phone intensively
- Likes to go out with her girlfriends
- Has many interests
- Considers herself to be creative
- Is interested in fashion
- Takes photographs in her spare time

Maria's goals:
- Find the profession of her dreams: one that is interesting, creative, and varied
- Get a degree in an interesting field of study that is varied and practically oriented
- Do something creative

»The more specific we make our personas, the more effective they are as design tools. [...] Giving the persona a name is one of the most important parts of successfully defining one. A persona without a name is simply not useful. Without a name, a persona will never be a concrete individual in anyone's mind.« Alan Cooper

1

»Personas are defined by their goals. Goals, of course, are defined by their personas. [...] Goals are the reason why we perform tasks. [...] Goals are not the same things as tasks. A goal is an end condition, whereas a task is an intermediate process needed to achieve the goal. It is very important not to confuse tasks with goals, but it is easy to mix them up. [...] Designing for tasks instead of goals is one of the main causes of frustrating and ineffective interaction. Asking, 'What are the user's goals?' lets us see through the confusion and create more appropriate and satisfactory design.« Alan Cooper

On the basis of the persona description of Maria Schneider and the definition of her goals, it is now possible to generate questions with which she will approach the Web material. Here the effectiveness of the method will become clear once again. Initially, it is not material from the viewpoint of the provider (that is, the college) that is made available; instead, a question is first defined that will find its answer afterwards only in the information provided by the college.

What might interest Maria? Naturally, the things that the course of study has to offer and the reputation of the college. However, at the same time, she also has completely different, much more personal questions that relate to her own situation. Maria also wants to know whether the course of study will suit her, whether she will like it, whether she can handle it at all, what awaits her when she begins her course of study, whether she will feel at home at the college, etc.

In addition, she wants to know in practical terms how such a course of study goes, how much work it involves, whether finding an apartment in the city could be a problem, and what there is to do there in her free time.

Putting oneself into the persona, seeing things through her eyes, and posing her questions regarding the Web site helps us, her—and the target group that she represents—to do a better job of meeting expectations.

Maria's questions are listed on the opposite page.

Maria has questions about the **Information Design course of study** and its contents:

- What is information design?
- What courses are there?
- Will the courses interest me?
- What does an actual course look like?
- Will this be fun?
- How much is theory and how much is practice?
- How much time will I have to devote to my studies?
- How many students are there in a seminar?
- Are there virtual classes? What are they like?
- What tests will I have to take?
- How long does the course of study take?
- What do others say about this course of study?
- Can I take a quick look at things?
- What abilities and skills will I have at the end of the course of study?
- What qualifications will I have at the end of the course of study?
- What can I do with my degree as a profession?
- How much money will I earn as an information designer?

In addition, she would like to find out some things about the **college** at which she will be spending the next few years:

- What is the quality of the college?
- What image does the college have?
- How qualified are the instructors at the college?
- How personable are the instructors at the college?
- How current is the instruction?
- What is the technical equipment of the college like?
- How do things look at the college?
- Will I feel at home there?
- Where exactly is the college located?
- What other college activities are there?
- Is there a student cafeteria?

And of course she has a few questions concerning her **application**:

- What are the prerequisites for applying?
- Must I present a portfolio?
- Is there a cap on admissions?
- How many people will be accepted?
- When is the deadline for applications?
- Do I have to pay tuition?
- Who will advise me and help me if I have questions?
- Where do I find the necessary forms?

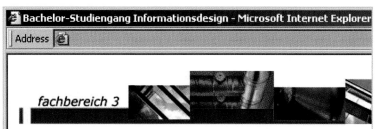

Looking for a course of study
that's creative and promises a
great future?

Based on Maria's goals and her
questions, the task now is to design
Web material that answers quickly
and satisfactorily her contextual
questions and her emotional questions (for example, »Will studying
be fun?«). These questions will be
answered not only by means of the
information that is offered, but also
through the manner in which this
information is offered (compare
here the chapter *Emotion*).

Maria must feel that she is being
addressed in many respects. She
must find her questions again and
receive the appropriate answers
quickly. The personas method helps
here to design the corresponding
pages.

Because there are also other personas besides Maria, it is important
to address specifically the various
target groups already on the start
page of the Web material and in
the appropriate area of the material
that is offered.

The examples show start pages which make clear that there are various specific areas for different target groups.

Here it is very important to speak the »language« of the particular target group. This means using both the text as well as images and the type of design to set an anchor that will be understood intuitively. The start page represents the entrance to the material that is being offered and is intended to invite the user to continue clicking.

The American designer David Siegel compares this to a restaurant where an inviting menu at the entrance ensures that the visitors' mouths start watering and that they will want to go into the restaurant. According to Siegel, the »fish food« should be scattered on the start page and an air of anticipation should be built up which this lure can then truly fulfill.

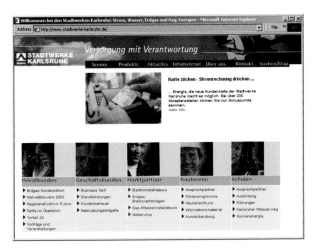

The material offered by the ALLIANZ INSURANCE COMPANY distinguishes on its *home page* between private customers and business customers and offers these two groups different material. The municipal utilities of the city of Karlsruhe, Germany, also guide different groups of people to various specially oriented offerings. And the AOL PUBLISHING COMPANY offers its material in a very specific manner (information for teachers, for parents and for students).

1.7 Which Product?

In addition to determining *for whom* you are creating your product, there is the question as to *what type* of a multimedia product is involved. This decision also influences the conception and implementation of your product substantially.

Multimedia information systems provide informational material on one or more specific topic areas. With your help, users want to get an overview of a topic or have pinpointed access to specific information. A typical example of this is an encyclopedia, such as MICROSOFT's *Encarta*.

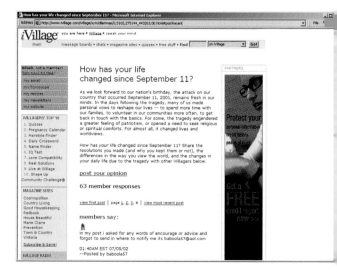

A new form of communication is provided by e-mail, chat rooms, and news groups. The use of e-mail has become established in universities and industry and is being used in people's homes more and more. The example shows a *message board*.

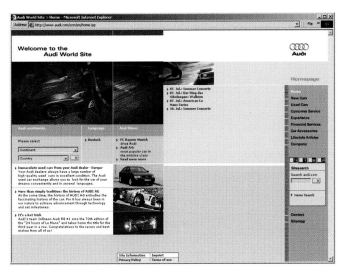

Advertising

For a few years now, companies have been using the World Wide Web intensively to advertise their products, with increasing success. Two aspects of this way of advertising are extremely attractive: especially the possibility to use interactive features cleverly (such as with customer surveys), and the relationship of cost and degree of effectiveness. The example shows the Audi portal.

Selling products over the Web has only just outgrown its baby shoes. Experts predict three-figure growth rates.

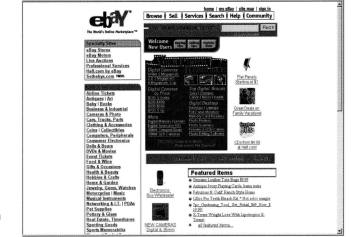

Virtual Communities are an attempt to combine the many communication capabilities of the Web with a social, personal level. This idea comes from Howard Rheingold and was first mentioned in his book of the same name in 1993.

A virtual community consists of members who are united by a specific interest. They provide information on this interest to other members. In some way, they feel responsible for the community and consciously contribute to the further development of the community.

The example shows the entrance to *Cybertown*.

Multimedia learning, at any time, in any place, and according to previous knowledge and individual need, becomes self-evident in the age of lifelong learning. The expectations placed on multimedia learning systems are high; however, they are fulfilled only if they are distinguished by a didactic concept that points toward the future. What is required here primarily are the motivation and strong activation of the learners. Training books on CD or on the Internet are not what is effective; rather, simulations and training systems that promote intensive communication of the learners. The example shows an international seminar on intercultural communication.

Experiencing

One of the most innovative areas is virtual reality, which by now enables simulations to have a very realistic effect. Thus, in this example, the imperial palace Ingelheim that was built by Charlemagne around 774 is made accessible again by means of computer animation. This anima-tion was based on material tests, ground plans, drawings, and photo-graphs of the ruins, as well as plans and designs of other pre-Roman buildings. The model is rendered to exact detail and reproduces the atmosphere of the imperial palace impressively.

Games

A large portion includes the group of games that appeal primarily to a young target group. The bandwidth is large and extends from reaction games to the complex adventure game. The example shows a screen shot from the game *Riven*.

1.8 Basics Checklist

☐ What goals do you want to achieve with your product?

☐ What target group(s) do you want to address?

☐ What kind of product are you dealing with (information system, tutorial, advertisement, etc.)?

☐ Have you defined personas? Are there dossiers for the personas?

☐ What are the goals of your personas?

☐ In what scenarios will the personas use your product?

☐ What »language« do your personas speak?

☐ What expectations do the personas have of what you have to offer?

☐ How can you »lure« your personas already on the start page and motivate them to continue clicking? What is the »bait?«

☐ Have you sketched the hypertext structure of your product on paper?

☐ Have you divided information and other material into manageable modules?

☐ Do you have an overall plan for your product?

☐ How does it fit in with other materials (such as printed brochures, manual)?

X

2 Orientation and Navigation

Multimedia hypertext systems are more like a space than a book. They can only be used effectively if they enable the user to have a clear orientation and simple navigation. This chapter provides methods and examples for facilitating orientation and navigation.

2.1 Where am I?

Disorientation Causes Insecurity

While most animals have a natural sense of direction and their ability to orient themselves to their surroundings is innate, we human beings do not have an orientation organ at our disposal. In spite of this, orientation to our surroundings is just as important to us and as necessary for survival as it is for the animals. Disorientation creates insecurity and can even lead to panic.

Orientation in Spaces

So, if we do not have an orientation organ, the question is, how do we manage to find our way around at all. In our familiar surroundings, we orient ourselves unconsciously by means of marked points and find our way in our homes, even in the dark. In unfamiliar surroundings, we look for orientation aids such as signposts or prominent features. Remember such situations as a lengthy hike through unknown territory, a visit to an unfamiliar city, to an airport terminal, or to a soccer stadium.

What goes on in our minds in such situations? Architects and psychologists have studied intensively what occurs and, in this context, they refer to **cognitive maps** that we create in our minds. This means that, in unfamiliar surroundings, we look for something familiar and form a rough picture of

how the place could be structured. In the course of our preoccupation with the unfamiliar surroundings, we refine our cognitive map more and more, revise it, discard parts of it, and rebuild it dynamically.

This cognitive map is not an objective representation of the location; rather, it is our subjective, individual impression of it. The map determines our behavior in the surroundings. The mental process of cognitive mapmaking described here is a very active process of permanent interpretation of the things which we perceive. And this process does not occur only where spatial orientation is concerned; rather, it occurs with every analysis of things, while learning, while dealing with human beings—we are always constructing a subjective impression of how things could be. We are always building our construct about human beings, topics, and places, and we believe that this is the way reality is. This process produces only our interpretation of

»As I was reading the hypertext, I often did not know how I was supposed to get back to where I had just come from.« Nielsen/ Lyngbaek 1990

»The main problem: the structure of the site did not meet the expectations of the users.« Spool et al. 1999

»The search for information in Web sites is a very frustrating experience.« Spool et al. 1999

our subjective perception, which is strongly influenced by previous experiences, emotions, interests, and expectations.

Lost in Hyperspace
Dealing with a hypertext system is also characterized strongly by human orientation behavior. Here, too, we look for orientation aids and construct a mental map of the »hyperspace.«

Of course, our perception of this space is extremely limited initially by the fact that we always see only a small section of it: always only one screen page.

Also absent for us is the use of other orientation sensors such as feeling our way around the space, or auditory aids, that is, orientation by sounds. It is as if we are wearing divers' goggles and are making our way through a large building, and we always have only

an extremely small field of vision. Our ears are closed and we have no possibility to touch anything; we are just traveling in a wheelchair. Not pleasant to imagine. But this is exactly the perception of many hypertext users.

The feeling of being lost in the network of the hypertext system with its abundance of links and navigation possibilities is familiar to most users of CD-ROMs and Web sites and is referred to as being *lost in hyperspace*. Hypertext that is not easy to follow (for example, a lot of Web sites) frustrates the user and he exits again quickly for this reason, as studies have confirmed (Spool et al. 1999).

In order to confront this lack of clarity and to provide the user with effective and rapid access to the information that is relevant to him, orientation and navigation aids are especially important. They have a function similar to that of directional signs in a subway station. They help the user to construct his cognitive map and in so doing facilitate considerably the understanding and use of the product. These aids give the user a feeling of security and motivate him to use the product properly. The following pages show possibilities for facilitating orientation and navigation.

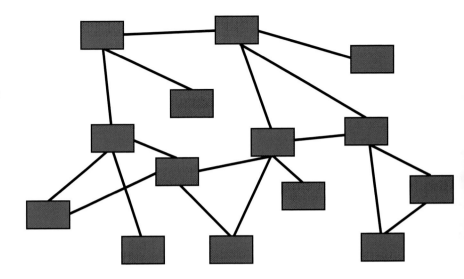

When planning your hypertext, you will facilitate access for the user if you put yourself into the situation of the user intensively, rather than basing you plan on the systematics of your topic or material. Consider the expectations and questions with which the user might approach your system, and the previous knowledge that he has. With reference to the general orientation and navigation in your system, the following questions are helpful.

Questions of the user about the multimedia product with reference to **orientation:**
- Where am I right now?
- What is the structure?
- Where all have I been?
- What all is available here?
- Have I seen everything? Have I overlooked anything important?

- Where is the information that is relevant to me?
- Will I be successful quickly?
- Is this fun or is it tedious?

Questions of the user about the multimedia product with reference to **navigation:**
- Where can I go? Which paths are available here?
- How do I get there?
- How do I get back? How can I trace back my path?
- How do I get out of here again quickly?

2.2 A Few Basic Questions

The user asks himself the following basic questions during his first contact with a CD-ROM or Web site:

- Who is the **sender**? From whom is the information coming? How authentic is the information?
- Who is the **addressee**? To whom is this supposed to appeal? For whom is the information intended? Is this suitable for me? Can I use this?
- What is the **topic**? What is it about? What contents are offered?
- How **current** is the information?

The first encounter with a Web site is similar to the first encounter with an unknown person. Instantaneously we form an opinion about who it probably is with whom we are dealing, whether we can trust this person, and what we can expect from this person.

Web sites should also answer these questions on the start page. The answers enable a new visitor to realize quickly whether it is worthwhile to continue working with the site. In this manner, trust is established.

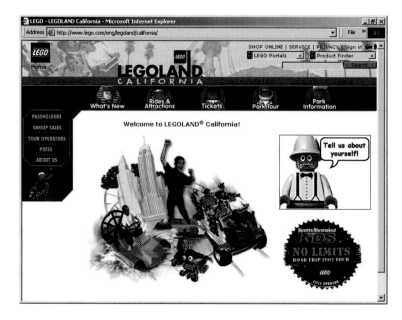

That the site comes from the LEGO Company is signaled not only by the text of the greeting, but also by the logo of the company and the presentation of the LEGO figures. That children are the target group is also clear here. The topic is the leisure park Legoland, which is advertised through games, information, and a virtual park tour.

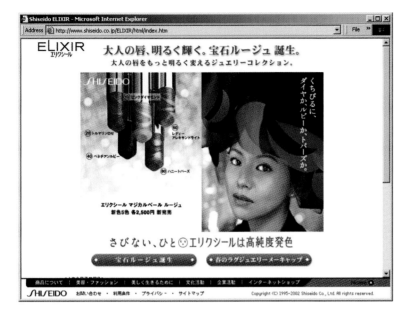

The sender is also recognizable here from the logo. The target group and the topics are signaled by means of pictures and color design.

With this start page, you have to look a little longer until it becomes clear that you have landed at NIKE USA. Only a modest logo in the picture and the printing at the lower right indicate this. What is it about? The navigation elements on the right margin provide information.

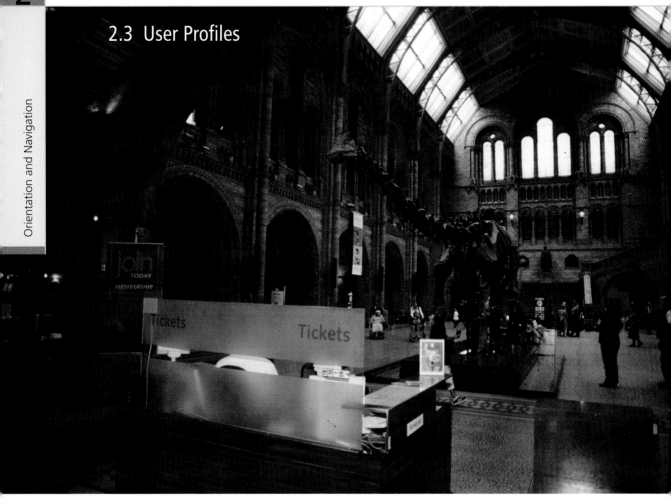

2.3 User Profiles

Methods of Access

Navigation in a hypertext system can be divided basically into three methods of access. The comparison to orientation and movement in a space is helpful here, too; for example, in a museum. In a museum, there are three types of visitors:

- Beginners
- Advanced visitors
- Experts

These three groups of people have different previous experience and intentions; they use the museum in very different ways. Let's take a look at these groups in detail.

The beginner visits the museum for the first time. His first question (at the entrance) is, perhaps, whether a visit to the museum is even worthwhile. In order to decide, he would like to know what awaits him in the museum, whether he has something to gain by visiting the museum because he might discover something useful or interesting and the visit might be fun for him. The first impression of the building and its atmosphere influence him in making this decision. Therefore the entry hall of the museum is an initial hurdle that he must jump, and the question is »What am I letting myself in for?«.

Once the visitor jumps the first hurdle, he attempts to orient himself quickly in order to find out what all there is in the museum and how it is arranged. Initially, the visitor pays less attention to the details; instead, he tries to get an overview. In seeking this overview, he is happy to find help, such as a guided tour that shows him the most interesting exhibits of the museum, or a marked path through the museum.

The advanced visitor is already familiar with the museum and knows what awaits him basically. In spite of this, there are still a lot of new things for him to discover. While doing so, he likes to »saunter« through the rooms, he looks at this and that, and he allows himself to be driven by his interests and the exhibits. He is helped by signposts and other orientation aids that indicate to him what is available where.

The expert knows the museum very well. He would like to look at extremely concrete exhibition pieces and investigate them closely and intensively. The expert has very specific interests, perhaps because he is looking for information on a particular topic. A guided tour would bore him. Also, he does not »saunter« through the museum; instead,

he zeroes in on specific places in the museum and selects exhibits that he wants to investigate.

This division into beginners, advanced visitors, and experts involves an ideal picture. However, we can assume that visitors to a museum as well as users of hypertext exchange these three roles flexibly. This division is intended to be an aid in understanding the use of a hypermedia system. In using a hypermedia system, paths and use vary greatly and require appropriate help.

So if you want to make the operation of your multimedia product easier for all three user groups, you should take into consideration the various methods of access and provide navigation and orientation aids.

Guided Tours for Inexperienced Users (Beginners)

For the beginner, the hypertext system and its topic are new. The first impression determines the evaluation of the system and whether it is worthwhile to investigate it further. For these reasons, elements that motivate the user are especially important; they are »bait« that lure him and direct him to investigate the system further. Otherwise, he is gone again quickly.

The basic attitude of the beginner is curiosity and a non-specific expectation, but also an insecurity as to how one can use the hypertext. An initial introduction in the form of a guided tour offers a lot of help.

General Plans for Advanced Users

The advanced user already has previous knowledge of the topic and how to use hypertext. For him it is especially important to get a total impression because he would like to know what all is relevant and whether he has seen the parts that are important to him.

His navigation behavior can be described with the terms »rummaging« or »sauntering.« In order to do this, he requires a clear representation of the structure of the hypertext and a lot of orientation aids. While the beginner likes to be guided, the advanced visitor walks through the hyperspace and even allows himself to be distracted from his path by interesting things. This phenomenon is called the *serendipity effect*.

Search Functions for Experts

The expert wants to call up the information that is relevant to him as quickly as possible from the hypertext. He is in a hurry and does not want any detours. For him, powerful search aids are necessary and useful.

Aids for All Three User Groups

So if you want to make the operation of your product easier for all three user groups, you should take into consideration the various methods of access and provide appropriate navigation and orientation aids.

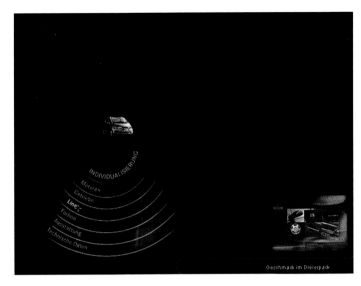

The CD *The New A-Class* from DAIMLERCHRYSLER set standards when it appeared. It uses a total overview to provide insight into the individual areas. Using this graphic overview, the user is able to understand the structure of the CD and to jump directly to the desired area.

With the *Encarta Encyclopedia*, an alphabetical listing of all related terms is displayed while the user types in the search term.

User	Basic Attitude	Questions	Needs	Motivation
Beginner	Curiosity	• What is going on here? • Does this interest me? • Can I use this? • What is the most important thing? • How does this work?	• Help for getting started • Motivation to continue working with the product • A marked path, the »guided tour«	• Attractive external appearance • »Bait« that encourages working with the product some more
Advanced visitor	Interest	• What all is available here? • Is there something new here for me? • Is this interesting and useful to me? • How is this structured?	• Overview of the areas of the product • Clear structures • »Maps«	• Elements that convey security in working with the product • Appealing navigation capabilities • Valuable, relevant information
Expert	Specific search	• Where do I find…? • Where can I find valuable information on the topic…?	• Search functions • Index	• Quick access to the object of the search

2.4 Wizards and Guided Tours

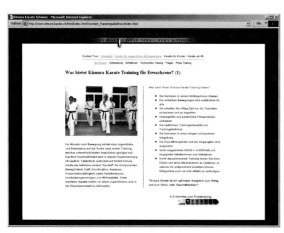

The example on the opposite page shows a guided tour through a karate school in Switzerland. First-time visitors are guided through the various stations of training presented clearly by means of text and images. This guided tour provides a good insight into the course of karate training at the sports school.

After a brief introductory text, the visitor is ready to go: initially, the visitor selects whether he would like to take a tour for adults, teenagers, children, or adults over 40. Then he »goes« step-by-step through the individual stations of the training. Finally, the Web site provides the opportunity to sign up for »real« test training.

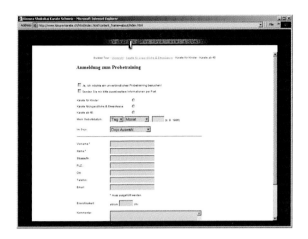

Wizards are valuable aides that are available as »personal advisors.« They explain or provide hints on how to operate a multimedia system. In one of the first information systems, the DAIMLER-BENZ Company used a wizard on their CD *The New E-Class*. She explains the individual stations of the CD and motivates the user to explore the CD. The video sequences of the spokesperson are integrated cleverly into the interface of the CD and allow you to skip over them if you want.

Russell Brown is the »wacky professor« of ADOBE SYSTEMS INCORPORATED who demonstrates his expert knowledge in short learning sequences of the picture-processing software *Photoshop*.

He also shows how to operate the program and he »divulges« his »secret« tricks. By means of his language and manner of presentation, he succeeds in establishing a personal, intimate atmosphere.

62

In order to appeal to a young target group, various identity figures are used on the CD *Please do not disturb*. Rather than being handled in a patronizing manner, questions about partnership, sexuality, and prevention are made a subject of discussion by »contemporaries« who inform in a very casual way.

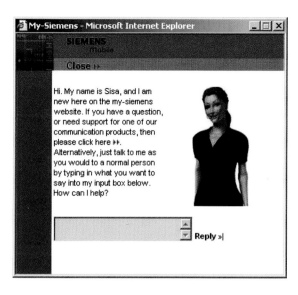

The digital wizards of the KIWI-LOGIC company react to natural language entries. Their mostly adequate answers and reactions lend them a personal note and give the Web site an emotional component. In addition to ARENA LEISURE and SIEMENS, other companies are in the meantime also using these »intelligent« advisors with success.

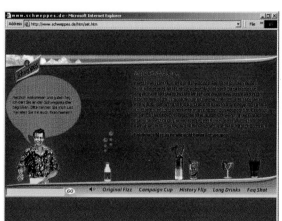

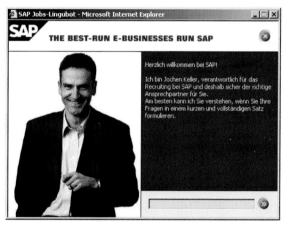

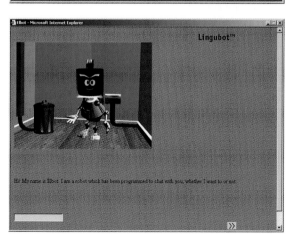

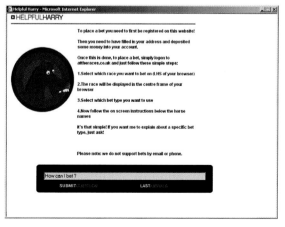

2.5 Metaphors

»A metaphor is a mental process by means of which we are able to understand something that lies beyond our capability to comprehend. With the help of the nearest thing that we master best, we can arrive at an understanding of the concept that is distant and difficult to grasp.« Ortega y Gasset

The Tasks of Metaphors

The use of a metaphor is a very effective and frequently used technique to make orientation and navigation in a multimedia product easier for users. A metaphor transfers something well known and familiar from the every day world of the user to the organization of data displayed on the screen. An example of this is the trashcan of the Mac OS that stands for the deletion of files.

Metaphors are effective because dealing with things that are familiar requires no further learning, and access to the multimedia product happens intuitively. Metaphors enable the user to perceive what is offered not as the sum of individual pieces of data, but to experience this offering as a unit.

However, one danger of metaphors is that they can eventually become pervasive if they are too dominant and can distract from the actual content.

The CD about the studios of HAL ROACH uses as metaphor the silver screen on which the old Laurel and Hardy films are shown and annotated.

Another metaphor: the chaos on the desk. This metaphor on an advertising CD of the WALT Company is not intended to facilitate orientation; rather, it is intended to make the user curious about all the things that he can find.

The metaphor travel diary uses the Swiss city of St. Gallen on its Web site. Navigation occurs by means of sticky notes that are stuck to various pages. Details such as torn pages or wine spots on the page of the diary strengthen the authenticity and liven up the presentation. The site is successful in keeping the metaphor consistent.

The CD-ROM *Opera Fatal* offers topics on the history of opera in the form of a search game. The user navigates through an opera house to research details for solving a crime. In so doing, he rummages around in old documents, he can listen to sound documents, and he becomes acquainted with the realms of the opera.

KinderCampus is a world of learning and experiencing for children that consists of various planets. In addition to the home planet, there are the most varied topic planets. The use of the space metaphor helps the children to click intuitively through the material that is offered. The examples on this page show the sport planet. Clicking on the various types of sports leads to educational, interesting information and activities in each case.

The children's encyclopedia *My First Incredible, Amazing Dictionary* of DORLINGTON KINDERSLEY works with a playing-card metaphor that is similar to the *Memory* game. An overview shows various cards, each covering one concept. Clicking on the concept calls up the corresponding (animated) information card.

The CD *Advertising in Motion* documents the history of the advertising film in a chronological sequence— in the form of a reel of film.

Characteristics of Suitable Metaphors

1. The metaphor should fit the topic and the content of the product. (Example: opera house as detective game about music)
2. The metaphor should be simple but, at the same time, not have a boring or trivial effect.
3. The metaphor should be familiar to the users. They should not have to put forth a lot of effort to work with the metaphor initially.
4. The more realistic the representation of the metaphor, the greater the acceptance by the user.
5. The visual representation of the metaphor should not dominate the actual contents; rather, it should transport them.
6. The metaphor should be multifaceted enough to be used in various situations.
7. The metaphor should be used uniformly and consistently in the product. Mixing of several metaphors causes confusion and destroys their effect.

2.6 Visual Orientation Elements

Using visual elements, such as colors or simple pictographs that are recognizable intuitively and quickly, provides a very good orientation aid. These elements should be clear, simple, and easy to remember. Text is suitable only under certain conditions, because it is not as easy to remember.

AMNESTY INTERNATIONAL uses the clear visualization of the topics of the start page (*Rights, Ideas, Stories, Voices, Places*) throughout its CD about human rights as background pictures for the corresponding sub-areas and in this way provides the users with clear signals as to where they are.

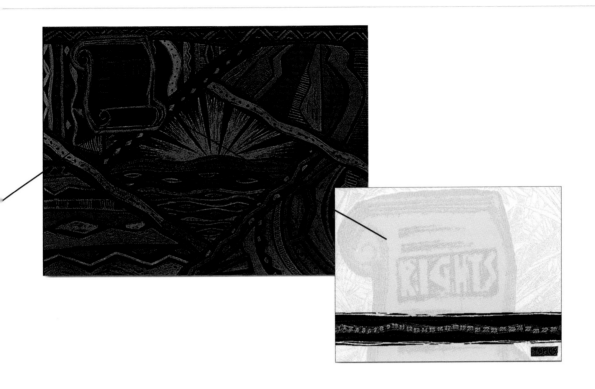

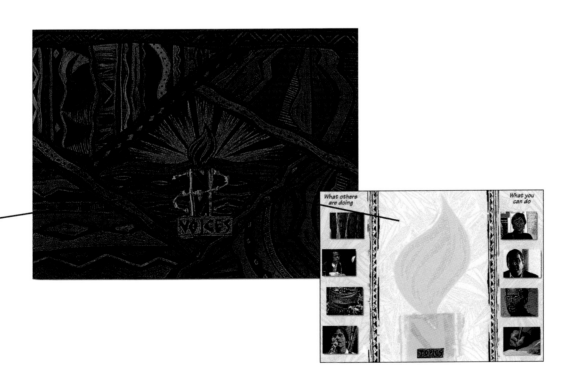

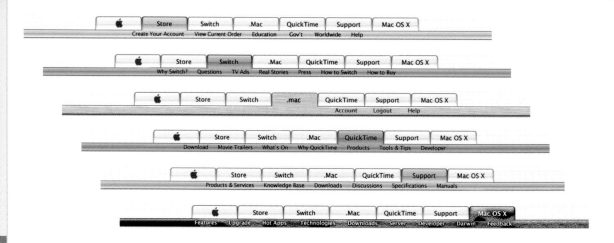

APPLE COMPUTER, INC. facilitates orientation on its Web site by using »riders« that are also highlighted with color.

The pages of YAHOO! indicate the navigation path, a very effective solution to orientation.

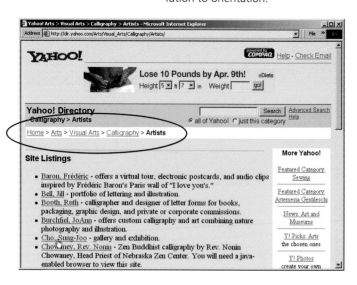

On the pages of the virtual BAUHAUS MUSEUM, color highlighting is carried through into the secondary areas.

2.7 Arrangement

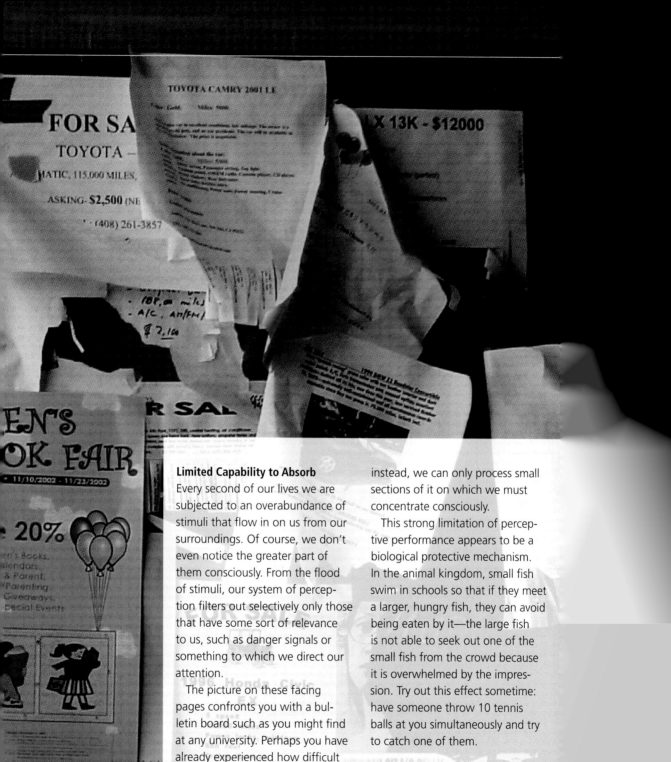

Limited Capability to Absorb

Every second of our lives we are subjected to an overabundance of stimuli that flow in on us from our surroundings. Of course, we don't even notice the greater part of them consciously. From the flood of stimuli, our system of perception filters out selectively only those that have some sort of relevance to us, such as danger signals or something to which we direct our attention.

The picture on these facing pages confronts you with a bulletin board such as you might find at any university. Perhaps you have already experienced how difficult it is to find your way around in this »flood of information.« We cannot process this excess simultaneously; instead, we can only process small sections of it on which we must concentrate consciously.

This strong limitation of perceptive performance appears to be a biological protective mechanism. In the animal kingdom, small fish swim in schools so that if they meet a larger, hungry fish, they can avoid being eaten by it—the large fish is not able to seek out one of the small fish from the crowd because it is overwhelmed by the impression. Try out this effect sometime: have someone throw 10 tennis balls at you simultaneously and try to catch one of them.

The Role of Short-Term Memory

An essential aid to promote orientation involves designing things simply and clearly, because the capacity of our ability to perceive and absorb is limited. Here our so-called short-term memory (= working memory) plays a central role. It processes the impressions of the outside world —absorbed by our sense organs.

The short-term memory has narrow boundaries. It can store its impressions only for a short time (up to approximately 15 seconds) and forgets them again later if they are not able to be processed and transferred to the long-term memory. In addition, the short-term memory can only store a limited number of information units: in a normal case, up to **seven units**. Then new impressions replace older impressions.

Surely you are familiar with the situation of looking up a telephone number from the telephone book so that you can call someone. You note the number and repeat it in your mind. Then if someone asks you something, for example, what time it is, you have forgotten the number again—your short-term memory has been overwritten by other information.

So if you want your users to be able to experience and comprehend the content of the screen as a unit, you must limit yourself and avoid providing too many elements.

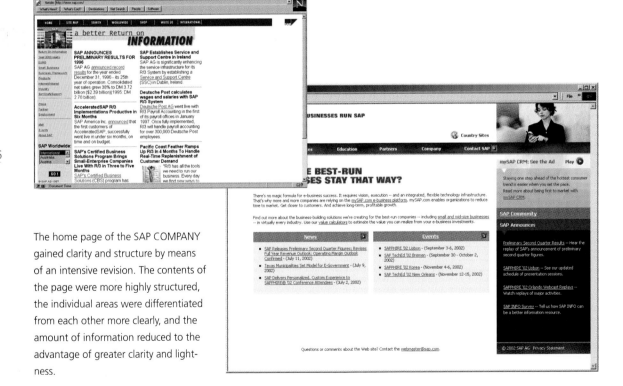

The home page of the SAP COMPANY gained clarity and structure by means of an intensive revision. The contents of the page were more highly structured, the individual areas were differentiated from each other more clearly, and the amount of information reduced to the advantage of greater clarity and lightness.

Chunks

The presentation of large amounts of information, complex contents, and long lists quickly becomes unclear for the user. To facilitate orientation and cognitive processing for the user, it is advisable to combine the information into logical groups. This process is called *clustering* or *chunking*.

Many search engines structure their complex offerings on the start page in this manner, as the examples on this page illustrate.

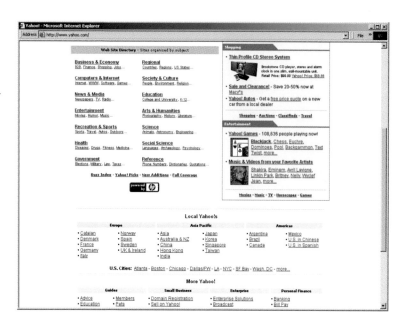

In this example, you see two lists—one without chunks, and one divided into groups. A small effect that achieves a lot.

2.8 Navigation Elements

Hypertext, or hypermedia, systems are distinguished by the fact that modules of information are linked to each other. Navigation takes place by means of clickable elements such as text (hot words), buttons, pictures, or parts of pictures (hot spots).

A basic question in the design of a multimedia system is whether elements for navigation, orientation, and content should be presented as strictly separated from each other or whether they should be woven together.

The site of the BRANDT COMPANY (above left) makes a clear visible separation between the navigation buttons and the information, while a CD-ROM on the topic of evolution (above right) mixes design and navigation with each other to such an extreme that the user first has to find out what the navigation elements are to begin with. The essential advantage of a clear separation is the rapid recognition of the navigation elements; the disadvantage lies in the fact that the relationship to the contents is not always clear and the willingness to navigate is reduced (Spool et al. 1999). Users also work more rapidly with hypertext if the links are integrated in the text (or on the visualized information) (Vora et al. 1994). Frequently the decision is to combine the two.

One essential requirement of navigation elements is that the user should be able to recognize what awaits him when he clicks on the navigation element. Show the user the goal. A link with the invitation »Click here!« will be accepted only by those of an extremely curious nature because, especially on the Web, users want to know what awaits them at the goal and how long it will take until they get there—that is, whether it is worth the effort.

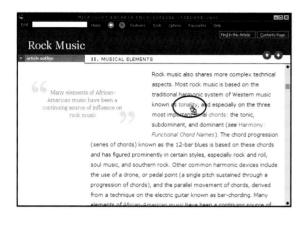

The most important navigation element in hypertext are the **hot words**. They can refer to places on the displayed page or also lead to other pages.

Hot words should live up to their name, that is, they should really be only single words or no more than short word groups because they are meant to catch the eye of the user. These words can be comprehended quickly and easily only if they are short.

Studies have shown that a lot of users call up hot words on Web sites more frequently than hot spots (images), that is, graphic navigation elements.

You should also really integrate hot words into the text. A separation of content and related links decreases usability considerably and therefore should be avoided.

The hot word should make clear where the link is going to take the user. Don't write »You can find additional information here.«. Instead, write »Read more in our current business report.«. In addition, on Web pages you can integrate a short explanation to the link and this explanation will be displayed by newer browsers.

In the example above (MICRO-SOFT *Encarta*), the hot words are marked in blue. If you want to make life easier for your users, use the standard of underlining words in blue (example *Encyclopedia.com*).

Hot spots are sensitive areas that react to clicking by the user. If they stand out from the background clearly and if the cursor changes when it touches them (for example, a change in the shape of the cursor, a change in the picture area, sound), it is easier for the user to recognize them as navigation elements.

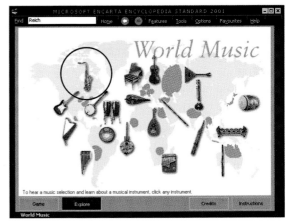

Drawers are groups of navigation elements that are displayed only as required. The children's CD *Max and the Secret Formula* uses a little cabinet as a drawer; when clicked on, a drawer comes out that contains the elements for navigation and other settings.

Buttons are frequently used as navigation elements. However, they often have a very »stiff« effect and are hard to integrate into the total design.

For the BUSINESS WEEK, the buttons turned out to be somewhat small; however, they are noticeable because of their striking color and they stand out from the rest of the content of the page.

Good navigation is distinguished by the following features:
- The navigation fits the goals, expectations, and behavior of the user.
- The navigation elements are not dominant. Navigation functions intuitively, without the user having to grapple with it or even learn it.
- The navigation elements are understandable immediately. The user does not have to learn to operate them. They are adapted to the topic.
- The navigation is consistent, that is, it is uniform throughout the product.
- The navigation provides the user with alternative ways to arrive at a goal.

2.9 Maps and Other Search Aids

Users of hypertext systems often have the insecure feeling of having overlooked important material.

A great preventive measure against this problem are overviews called **site maps**. They visualize the structure of the hypertext and indicate the structure of a Web site in the form of an overview graphic or a structured list of key words. A prerequisite to understanding this structure is that the product has been designed from the viewpoint of the potential user, not from the viewpoint of the person who created the Web site.

For example, a Web site that reflects the internal structure of a company is not very helpful to a user who would like to find out something about the products of this company. The structure must be easily transparent to the user and also must correspond, in the type of presentation and in concept, to his previous experiences.

In addition to providing an overview, site maps also often enable an effective type of navigation by allowing the user to click on a topic or icon on the map to get to the corresponding location.

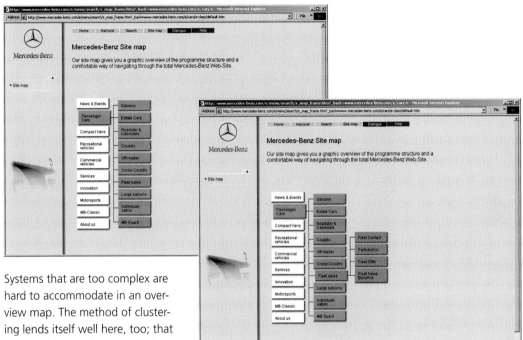

Systems that are too complex are hard to accommodate in an over-view map. The method of clustering lends itself well here, too; that is, combining topics into a higher-level topic. On the Web site of MERCEDES-BENZ, the user can call up the appropriate secondary topics by clicking on one of the ten main topics. This summarized overview makes it possible to represent the site's total of 115 topic modules clearly.

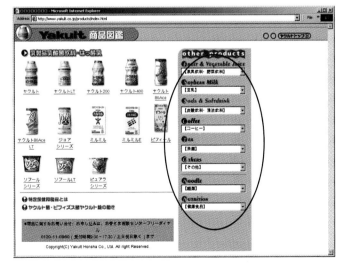

On the YAKULT site, so-called *drop-down boxes* are used for navigation. This practice initially reduces the number of selection elements to eight main areas whose secondary areas can be selected individually.

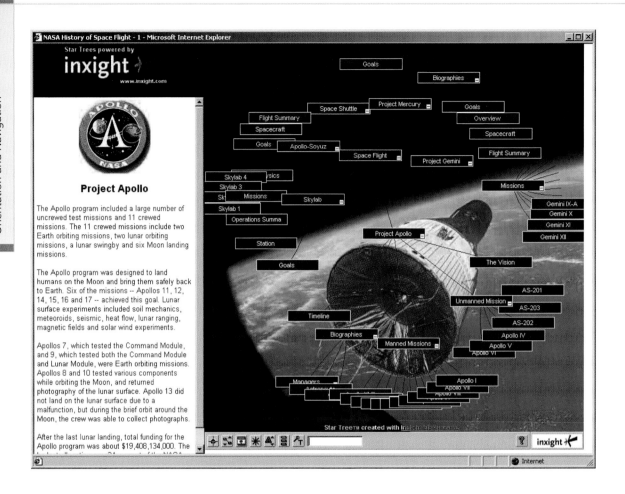

A very innovative and flexible type of map is implemented in the **Star Tree** of the INXIGHT Company.

This dynamic presentation of the mindmap-type structure of complex hypertext demonstrates above all the rough structure and the main topics. When you select a main topic, the corresponding secondary topics appear; if you click on a secondary topic, additional subtopics appear. The user experiences the hierarchy as a space whose areas can be zoomed in.

The orientation in the entire space is preserved and, at the same time, access to detailed areas is possible without losing the context. The example in the illustration shows the historical overview of NASA with the help of the Star Tree.

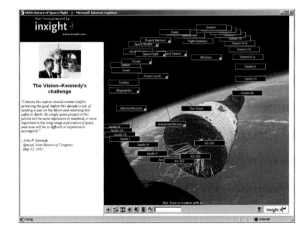

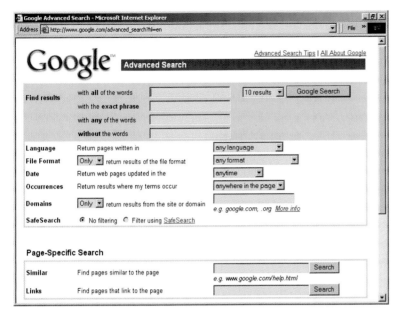

The **search function** is another valuable aid for the person who knows exactly what he is looking for. Please note that, in any case, you should incorporate the capability of masking functions with wildcard characters, for example, with the entry of »children*«, you can get search results such as »children's schools,« »children's diseases,« and »children's games.« Boolean operators should also be a possibility (such as logical AND operations, logical OR operations).

A more transparent form is an **index**, which lists all key words alphabetically. The user sees which key words can be selected.

2.10 Orientation and Navigation Checklist

☐ Can the user identify clearly who created the product?

☐ Is there an imprint or copyright notice?

☐ Is it possible to contact the creator of the product?

☐ Can the user identify clearly when the product was created (indication of date)?

☐ Based on the contents and design of the start page, can the user determine the topic (or topics) of the product intuitively? Can the user easily recognize the type of product that is involved (information system, tutorial system, game, etc.)?

☐ Can the user already evaluate the personal practicality of the product *before* he has worked with it intensively?

☐ What does the user expect from your product?

☐ What previous knowledge does the user have?

☐ Can the user recognize what previous knowledge and other prerequisites (for example, of a technical nature) are assumed?

☐ Does the user have the possibility of looking at prominent areas of the product by means of a guided tour?

☐ Are the areas of the product clearly recognizable to the user in an overview?

☐ Is there a site map?

☐ Does this site map make it possible to navigate directly to the individual areas of the product?

☐ Is there a search function?

☐ Does the search function provide differentiated selection (*Boolean operators*)?

☐ Is there an index?

- [ ] Can the user trace his way back on the path that he took?

- [ ] Can the user set *bookmarks*?

- [ ] Is it possible for the user to recognize where he is in the system at any given time?

- [ ] Can the user return to the start page at any time?

- [ ] Are there Help functions to support the user when he has problems with the navigation or orientation?

- [ ] Is a wizard provided?

- [ ] Will this wizard be accepted by the target group? Is it »sympathetic« to the target group?

- [ ] What are the concrete tasks of the wizard?

- [ ] Is a metaphor used?

- [ ] Is the metaphor used consistently throughout the product?

- [ ] Is the metaphor »purposeful« and not dominant?

- [ ] Is the metaphor familiar to the target group?

- [ ] Does the metaphor fit the topic of the product?

- [ ] Is the metaphor multifaceted enough to avoid being ineffective?

- [ ] How do you show the user where he is within your hypertext system?

- [ ] How do you make the structure of your system clear to the user?

2

☐ Which visual orientation elements (graphics, text, colors, etc.) are used?

☐ Do you apply your orientation elements consistently?

☐ Are auditory orientation elements provided?

☐ Which visual and textual navigation elements are used?

☐ Are the navigation elements used consistently?

☐ Is the labeling or visual design of the individual navigation elements understandable to the user?

☐ Are the orientation and navigation elements clearly recognizable in their function?

☐ Are the standard orientation and navigation elements available on all pages?

X

3 Information

How should information be prepared so that it can be used appropriately for digital media? How do people read at a monitor? How do you create suitable and understandable texts? What do you need to keep in mind when using pictures, videos, and animation? This chapter shows how to prepare content that is appropriate for the medium.

3.1 Reading Text on a Monitor

Reading a Screen Is an Effort

Reading text from a monitor is more strenuous and more unpleasant than reading printed text. Tests have shown that the speed for reading something on the screen is 25–30% slower and that the reader reads with less concentration and less accuracy.

There are various reasons for these findings. An essential reason appears to be the low resolution of characters on the monitor. This low resolution makes it more difficult to comprehend words quickly. In addition, the »flickering« of the

CRT monitor has a tiring effect on the eyes, as does the fact that the user is looking into a source of light (while with paper, he sees reflected light).

It also has been shown that people who work at screens tend to assume a very stiff sitting posture and »stare« at the monitor; that is, they tend to blink (an action that moistens the eyes) less frequently. The conclusions of these findings are that the majority of people avoid reading text from a monitor, either consciously or unconsciously.

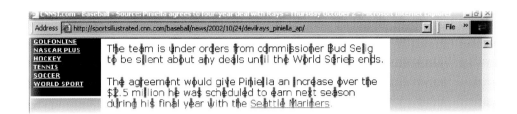

Saccades and Fixations

When we read, our eyes do not capture the individual letters of a text continuously; instead, they jump over the text (saccadic eye movements), fixate on text locations (fixation), and in so doing capture the words to the left and right of the fixation point. During this fixation, word recognition takes place, resulting in the comprehension of information.

Reading is very different for different readers. For those who do not read much, for example, the saccades are shorter than for those who read a lot, and the fixations last longer. In addition, those who read a lot jump back in the text less frequently. Reading a text by means of relatively large saccades and relatively short fixations, but during which the information can be comprehended appropriately, appears to be the most effective reading. In these matters, of course, no guiding values can be specified because the type of text, the mood and surroundings of the reader, and other factors play an additional role.

However, the important point here is the realization that reading a text can be made more difficult or easier by means of its content as well as its presentation. This fact plays a big role where printed media are concerned; however, it is probably perceived by readers unconsciously. Where reading from a monitor is concerned, this fact is more significant. For this reason, screen designers should strive toward an optimization of text in order to facilitate the comprehension of information. This optimization will increase the acceptance and usability of information offered on a Web site or a CD.

So to facilitate reading, you have to prepare text in a manner that is suitable for a monitor. This means that the text must be optimized in its scope (not much text), in its presentation (typography), and in its contents (semantics).

The illustration shows the fixations of a reader while reading text on a screen.

3.2 Screen Typography

»The browser companies make good typography more than a challenge. They continue to make it near impossible.« David Siegel

Unpredictable, Inflexible, Qualitatively Useless

For designers and especially typographers, interactive media are not only a challenge, but also agony. While quality standards have been formulated for printed media, and professional layout presents contents appropriately, typographers have to put up with serious limitations with CD-ROMs and Web pages.

First of all, there is the limited resolution of the computer monitor—in comparison to printed matter. In addition, the producer of interactive media can influence the material that the user sees on the screen only within certain limits. Each screen has a different color temperature, a different contrast, a different brightness, and a different ambient light. The designer of a Web page does not know what resolution or what screen size the user employs, nor does he know what fonts the user has installed in his operating system. And then again, if the designer uses certain standard Windows fonts as a basis, things will look different for those users who own a Macintosh or a Linux system. And also, if fonts are

integrated on a CD-ROM as graphics, the screen size can have a great influence on the presentation.

In spite of these limitations, it is important to master the basics of typography and—to the greatest extent possible—to take them into consideration when designing screens. And in the meantime, with the help of cascading style sheets, you can apply typographic rules to Web pages to a certain extent.

Permanently set font in the browser: Arabia.

Scr

Serif font
Sans serif font

In typography, one distinguishes between serif fonts and sans serif fonts. Serifs are the little hooks and curlicues on the letters. Among other things, they help to distinguish the individual letters from one another and they lend a specific character to each letter. This effect becomes especially clear in comparison to sans serif fonts as illustrated in the example of the word »Illusion,« whose first three letters cannot be distinguished from one another in this sans serif font.

Because of these specific characteristics, serif fonts are generally more comprehensible and more legible in the realm of printed media. For this reason, this type of font is used in the majority of printed books and periodicals.

On the screen, on the other hand, sans serif fonts are more suitable because fine serifs cannot be displayed well in the limited screen resolution. For this reason, sans serif fonts are more suitable. Only above a certain size (depending on the font, starting with 16 points), can serif fonts be displayed without any problems.

Anti-Aliasing

You can increase the legibility of screen fonts considerably if you present the font with the help of anti-aliasing. This is a technique that eliminates the stairstepping effect (*aliasing*) that results because fonts are represented by means of pixels on the screen. This effect is especially noticeable in an enlargement, as the upper letter shows in the illustration on the right. However, with a font size under 10 points, anti-aliasing font representations are hardly legible.

The anti-aliasing technique creates smooth transitions on the edges of the letters (as shown in the lower letter on the right). You can use almost all image-processing programs to create fonts with anti-aliasing.

Myriad: Fonts that are optimized for the screen are distinguished by clear shapes and curves and have a relatively wide span.

Minion: Fonts that are optimized for the screen are distinguished by clear shapes and curves and have a relatively wide span.

Verdana: Fonts that are optimized for the screen are distinguished by clear shapes and curves and have a relatively wide span.

Georgia: Fonts that are optimized for the screen are distinguished by clear shapes and curves and have a relatively wide span.

Coinn: Fonts that are optimized for the screen are distinguished by clear shapes and curves and have a relatively wide span.

Fonts for the Monitor

Fonts that have clear and simple shapes are especially well suited. Various vendors offer font types that are optimal for use on the screen. Such fonts are, for example, *Myriad* and *Minion* from ADOBE or the TrueType fonts *Verdana* and *Georgia* from MICROSOFT that are integrated in the newer versions of Windows.

Another extremely interesting font type for the monitor is *Coinn*, developed by Jan Jedding at the BREMEN COLLEGE OF ARTS. It is distinguished by good use of space and has a very well balanced and harmonious effect.

Illustration on the right-hand page: Most font types make a certain statement by means of their specific characteristics and can »communicate« seriousness, frivolity, transience, or tradition through their presentation alone. The opposite page illustrates quite clearly how a statement can be neutralized by using an unsuitable font type.

Yesterday afternoon on Highway A3 there was a tragic rear-end collision. The police reported ten people seriously injured and three dead.

Our life insurance policies are a solid basis for your old-age pension. Our insurance provides international coverage.

Dear Peter. I would like to invite you to join me in celebrating my fourth birthday. We will play in the yard and eat cake.

Our company works with the latest technology and has a corporate culture that is geared toward the future and progress.

The Western Club DAKOTA has extensive, wonderfully situated club grounds.

The newest science fiction film of successful director Dieter Müller takes the audience into an unknown galaxy and shows scenes that no one has ever seen before.

With this message I would like to inform you that you are fired. The serious errors of the last few days are inexcusable. We've had enough!

Life in harmony with nature is for us a life that renounces all technology.

Flush Left instead of Justified

Left-justified, ragged right para-graphs are easier to read than text that is justified (aligned evenly along both the left and right mar-gins of a column), for which spaces of different sizes are inserted between words to maintain the alignment. Right-justified text is ex-tremely problematic. Centered text should only be used in exceptional cases (such as in a short heading).

Line Spacing (Leading)

The spaces between lines (leading) should be larger on the screen than on paper. Too small a space makes it considerably more difficult to read the text; too large a space tears vi-sual holes in the text. For texts that are to be read on a monitor, spac-ing of one and one-half to two lines is recommended for running text. The spacing in headings can be somewhat narrower.

Paragraphs

Leave some additional space be-tween individual paragraphs to set them apart from each other clearly. This method enables the reader to perceive paragraphs as »visual units« (*visual chunks*).

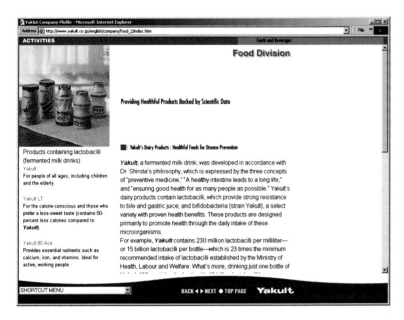

Air

Give your text »air.« Let it breathe, that is, give the eye empty spaces that can serve as resting points. In this manner, your text will gain more attention, will be more legible, and will have a more meaningful effect.

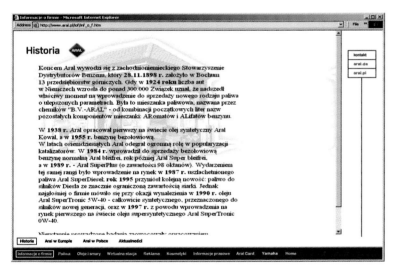

Using background pictures

does have an elegant effect at first glance; however, it usually makes reading more difficult. This is the case primarily when the background is too dominant and the contrast between the background structure and the text that is placed upon it is too small. The text should stand out clearly enough from the background. One way you can achieve this goal is by using the milk-glass effect, as shown in the example to the left. Additional softening of the background can increase this effect.

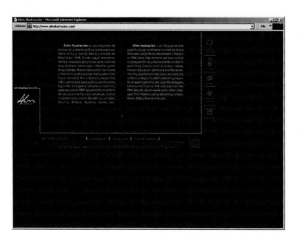

The **contrast** of the color of text to the color of its background has a considerable influence on legibility. A high contrast makes reading easier, while medium contrasts are perceived as especially pleasant. If the contrast is too small, reading becomes much more difficult.

Using a very saturated color as the background color results in the background being too dominant and possibly distracting from the text. Let the background really step »into the background,« for example, by using unsaturated colors and unobtrusive pastel tones.

Note also the significance of the colors that are described in the next chapter. Text colors should not be used for their own sake or as decoration; rather, they should underscore information.

The two examples above show too little contrast, which makes reading very difficult. The two examples below present the problems associated with a dominant background—warm and vivid colors.

The color combination red-green should definitely be avoided. Because of the different wavelengths of these colors, the eye has difficulty focusing on each color and seeing each one clearly.

green on red

red on green

3.3 Writing Text for the Monitor

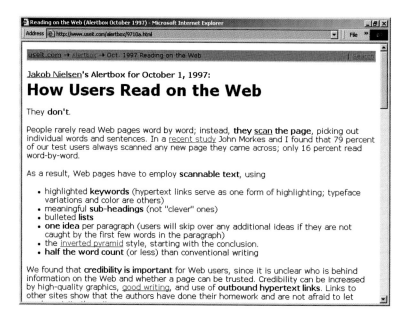

Scannable Text

The question as to how people read text on a screen was answered by the American Web researcher Jakob Nielsen with the clear statement »They don´t«, and then he added: People scan (that is, skim through) screen text.

As already mentioned, reading on a screen is strenuous, and people tend to avoid this strenuous activity and to read little on a screen. That is to say, most people print out relatively long texts as opposed to reading them on a monitor. This fact should have consequences for screen designers.

Scannable text is distinguished by brevity and conciseness. It has a clear structure both visually and contextually and, because of this, it can be comprehended quickly. This text is created especially for the screen and it is devoid of frills. It is supplemented by pictures, graphics, and hyperlinks and makes reference to longer passages of text that have been edited for printing out.

```
IDEEN - DAS BUCH LE GRAND                283


Chapter XII

The German censors – – – – – – – – – – – – – – – – – – – – – – – –
– – – – – – – – – – – – – – – – – – – – – – – – – – – – – – – – –
– – – – – – – – – – – – – – – – – – – – – – – – – – – – – – – –
– – – – – – – – – – – – – – – – – – – – – – – – – – – – – – – –
– – – – – – – – – – – – – – – – – – – – – – – – – – – – – – – –
– – – – – – – – – – – – – – – – – – – – – – – – – – – – – – – –
– – – – – – – – – idiots – – – – – – – – – – – – – – – – – – – –
```

The German poet Heinrich Heine wrote an early scannable text passage in his *Travel Pictures*. He caricatured the censorship prevalent in 19th century Germany by not blackening out the few relevant words of his text.

Characteristics of Scannable Text
- In total, little text
- One idea per paragraph
- Short, concise paragraphs with expressive heading
- The use of the inverted pyramid style
- Highlighted keywords
- Structured visually
- Use of lists and tables
- Clear, understandable language
- Integration of images, video, animation, and sound
- Separation of text for the monitor and text to be printed out

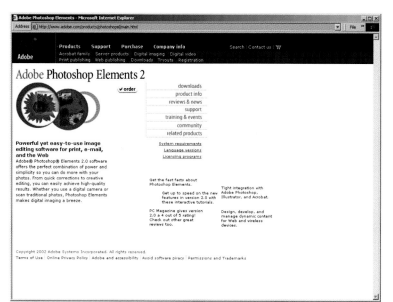

Little Text

The examples show the proper use of text on Web pages. The amount of text shown is still acceptable for display and reading on a screen. The page divisions all have a certain »effortlessness« that facilitates reading. The statements of the text are supplemented by pictures and additional hyperlinks. This presentation makes the pages and text easy to comprehend and manage.

One Idea per Paragraph

Write your text that is suitable for the screen briefly and concisely, and clarify the contextual (semantic) structure visually, too, by giving each thought or topic its own paragraph.

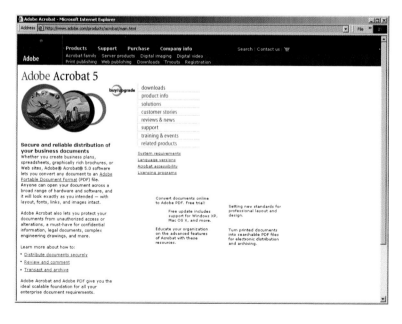

Expressive headings

summarize the text and allow the reader to decide whether the content of the text could be relevant and interesting.

Relatively long text passages should have subheadings that structure the text contextually and visually. Highlight the headings in such a way that they are eye-catching.

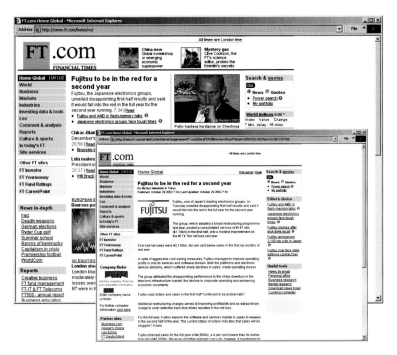

Write in the Inverted Pyramid Style

Text passages that use the inverted pyramid style begin with a concise summary of the information that follows. This style of writing is familiar from newspapers: heading—summary—details.

In the example from the FINANCIAL TIMES, the start page displays short teasers from actual articles that can be called up by means of a link.

CNN Online also uses short introductory text passages, here highlighted in boldface type.

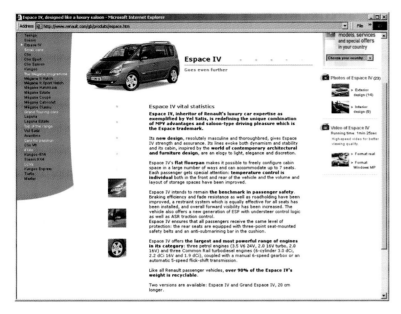

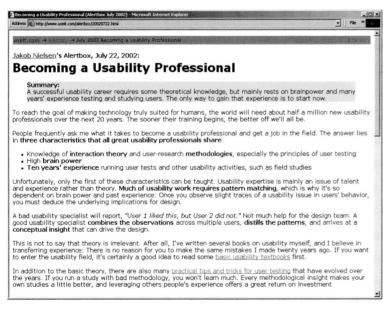

Highlighted Keywords

Keywords are words that make it possible to understand a text passage without reading the other words. Keywords that are highlighted with boldface type enable the reader to skim the text (scanning).

On this page you see two good examples of using keywords. But be careful: keywords are rarely names or technical terms, for such words rarely summarize a text passage.

A simple test can determine whether you have chosen the right keywords: give someone only the keywords to read. If, afterwards, the person knows what the text passage is about, then the keywords are appropriate.

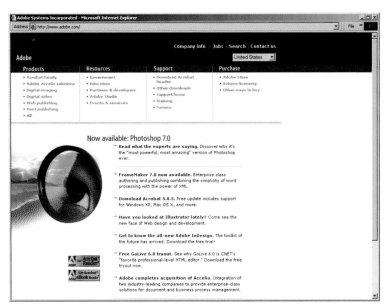

Visual Structure

The more order and structure you offer to the reader, the simpler it is for him to find his way around and to comprehend the contents of a page quickly. For this advantage, the reader will be very grateful.

At the same time, a visual order suggests—and you shouldn't underestimate this—the feeling of seriousness, reliability, and trustworthiness.

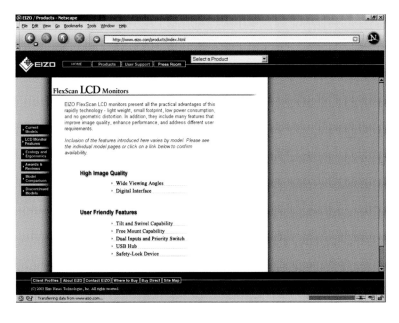

Use Lists

Lists, tables, and other visualizations of structures give your text an arrangement that makes it clear. In the example on the left, this clarity is achieved by means of the bulleted lists, the bold headings, and the indentations.

Write Concisely, Clearly, and Understandably

Use sentences that are short and limited to that which is essential. Use language that is clear, concrete, and graphic. Formulate your sentences so that they are varied and stimulating. Explain technical terms (by using a hyperlink) and take into consideration the existing knowledge of your potential reader. Write as little as possible, but not less than necessary.

This is not so simple, but the effort is worthwhile because your reader notices right away whether you have simply taken your text directly from printed media or whether you have created it especially for the screen.

Understandable Text

»Difficulty in understanding is based less on the "what" than on the "how," not on the content, but on the form of the text.« (Langer/Schulz v. Thun/Tausch 1993, 10)

In this context, understandable text is distinguished by the following features:

1. **Simplicity**
   Simple sentence structure and clear choice of words facilitate understanding of text, as does concrete and clear language. Technical terms should be explained.

2. **Organization—Arrangement**
   A clearly structured, logical inner arrangement of a text passage that is reflected in the external organization is ideal. This method should differentiate clearly that which is essential from that which is not, and the »marked path« should be visible.

3. **Brevity—Conciseness**
   The feature of conciseness concentrates on the essential part of the content and on the goal that is supposed to be achieved with the text.

4. **Stimulating Supplements**
   Concrete examples make the text clear and varied.

Use Multisensory Forms of Presentation

Structures and relationships can be presented well by means of pictures; procedures by means of animation or video sequences; short, accompanying introductions by means of sound and music. Use these possibilities appropriately and develop an effective combination of different multimedia elements. Because of the limited transmission capacities of the WWW, you should only use elements such as animation, video, and sound as options.

The example from the RENAULT Company shows very nicely how the descriptive text is supplemented by photos and video sequences that you can call up. The visual elements are listed and described briefly in a column on the right margin of the screen.

For the videos, the user can select the desired format and is informed about the run time. In addition, the user gets control elements that enable him to control the sequence of the video.

An effective media mix is—in addition to the hypertext structure—the strength of digital encyclopedias, such as *Encarta*.

After a short »teaser,« the reader of the MIAMI HERALD can look at the complete article. The important print function leads to a page that contains only pure text and images.

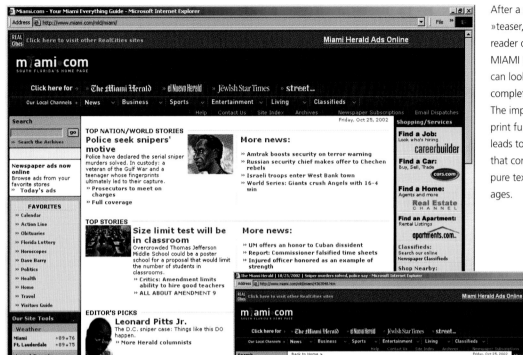

Distinguish between short text passages that will be read on the screen and text passages that will probably be printed out. The longer text passages should be optimized for print output, that is, they should contain no »frills« if possible, such as navigation elements and advertising banners. A good option for text intended for printing is to offer an extra page, as shown in the example on this page. Also the use of the PDF format from ADOBE lends itself to this purpose.

The example shows a possible sequence:

1. Short, concise summary
2. Detailed text
3. Printable text

3.4 Scrolling

The capability to use the mouse to move the screen content or a part of it vertically (sometimes horizontally also) is called *scrolling*. Often, scrolling seems to be the only possibility to accommodate a relatively long text—or a relatively large picture—on the screen.

Studies have shown that users really dislike scrolling, they read scrolled text more slowly, and they have problems processing the content of the information in scrolled text. With relatively long pages, users often lose the context and have to remember too much information that is not visible. Even if scrolling has gained acceptance in recent years, it is problematic now as ever. If you can avoid scrolling, you should. Otherwise, you should make sure that you place the most important information in the upper area of the screen that is visible initially, because this area is noticed the most. In addition, you should give the scrollable text the clearest and most visually noticeable structure. Use concise titles, short paragraphs, and supplementary graphics. Within the text, also provide the user the capability of jumping back to the starting point of the page.

You should avoid horizontal scrolling in any case.

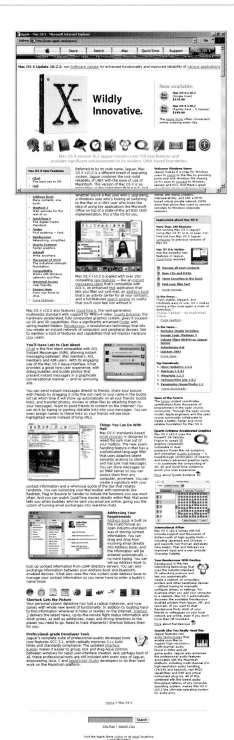

The home page of APPLE makes clear how designing a page for a specific screen resolution (600 x 800 pixels) can increase its clarity of arrangement: first, the user sees compact information and motivating elements, and only then comes to the actual facts by scrolling the page. With higher resolutions, this elegant separation no longer works.

As an alternative, the designer could have implemented this separation by using an additional page.

In the example below, the topic *History of the Advertising Film* has also been visualized consistently with the scroll bar (in the form of a filmstrip). For a thematically clear CD-ROM, this is surely a good possibility. However, the user here must re-learn how to operate the scroll bar. For this reason, you should normally resort to the standard elements of the operating system or browser.

113

3.5 »A Picture Is Worth More Than a Thousand Words«

»Pictures, because they look like the things they represent, require less mental effort to translate between referent and reality. Pictures give information that is more familiar and easy to process, and this may promote more passive thinking.« Byron Reeves/Clifford Nass

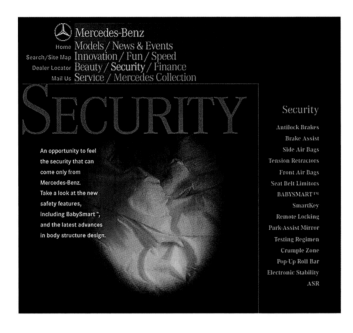

Next to text, pictures are the most important information elements in a multimedia system. In contrast to text, pictures »jump« into view immediately and are perceived more rapidly than text. What did you see first when you initially glanced at the screen shot above? Probably the sleeping child.

Studies have confirmed what the advertising business has known for a long time: people react to pictures intensively and quickly. Pictures are compelling, »fast shots into the brain,« as the consumer and behav-

ioral researcher Werner Kroeber-Riel said. A few facts:

- The topic of a clear, lucid picture can be recognized in 1/100 of a second.
- We can remember a very large number of pictures; that is, our memory capacity for pictures is considerably greater than for text.
- Pictures are processed with less mental exertion.
- Our memory performance is increased by pictures.
- Pictures have a very great, often unconscious, influence on our behavior.

Of course, pictures are normally not perceived immediately as intensively as it appears. For this reason, they can lead to superficial perception. Many elements of a picture are recognized only unconsciously or not at all, although we have the feeling that we »understood« the picture. But did you see the Mercedes star in the picture? If not, then look again closely.

We remember pictures better not only because they appeal to our visual system of perception, but primarily because they code information differently than text. Linguists refer to **symbol systems** that they divide into three different systems: pictures, numbers, and language. These symbol systems organize and structure their information in very different ways. While the symbol system *language* proceeds sequentially and linearly, the symbol system *picture* presents all information simultaneously. (Films and videos, by the way, are assigned to the picture symbol system. At the same time, however, they also have a sequential aspect of narrative through the linear succession of pictures.) This means that the same information is also presented differently in different symbol systems. Some text (such as directions to a location) allows itself to »come to the point« with the help of a picture and be presented clearly and lucidly. Other text (such as legal or philosophical text) cannot be visualized so easily.

The practicality of multimedia surely lies in the skillful and sensible combination of picture and text, as well as sound, video, and animation. This means that contents can be presented with the help of various media and symbol systems that complement each other.

For example, a text describes abstract relationships, a picture shows a structure, and a video clarifies a

procedure. Added to this is also the possibility of interaction, that is, the targeted selection of further details.

3.6 Three Functions of Pictures

Basically, pictures in multimedia products have **three functions** that are shown here with the help of the *Encarta Encyclopedia* from MICROSOFT:

- Illustrating
- Structuring
- Motivating

Mixing these functions can be done only with difficulty.

For this reason, decide consciously when you want to inform, when you want to use pictures to structure your product, and when you want to use pictures motivationally as decoration.

1. The **illustrative function** consists of supplementing the textual and linguistic contents. The picture has a relationship to the contents and shows something that the text describes.

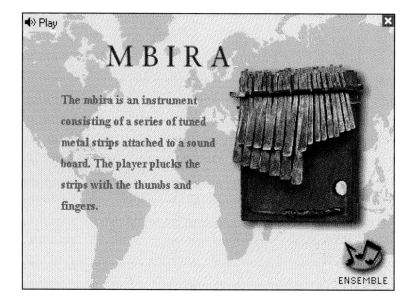

2. The **structuring function** visualizes the structure of a topic. It shows an arrangement. In addition, this function can serve as orientation and is popularly used as a navigation element.

3. The **emotional function** forms the emotional attitude to the actual contents. An aesthetic context that is of high quality and is attuned to the topic motivates the user and inspires trust. If pictures are used only as decorative elements without the intention of communication, they lose their positive effect quickly.

3.7 Pictures That Work

Multimedia products live from photos and
graphics. A few suggestions for the effective
use of images follow.

Get Up Close

Get close to what you want to
show. Emotionally, too. Captivate
the viewer with something eye
catching, not with a collection of
details.

Reduce to the Essential

You don't have to show everything.
Hints are totally adequate if they
can be understood by the viewer.

Combine the Familiar and the Unknown

By combining something familiar with the unknown, you arouse curiosity. Surely no one expects a sacred motif on the promotion CD of the ANTWERPES & PARTNER agency.

Knowing that this agency is located in the cathedral city of Cologne makes one even more curious.

Not All Sorts of Colors, but Colorful

Most good photos don't have a jumble of colors; instead, they are colorful. That is, they use colors selectively, in a focused manner, and ones that match each other.

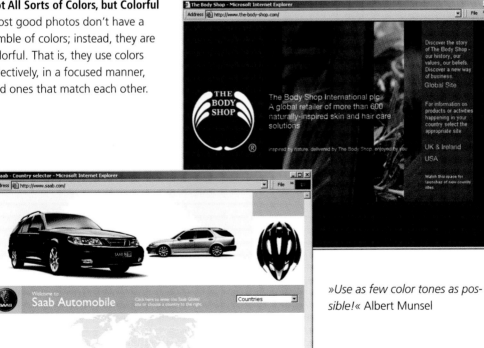

119

»Use as few color tones as possible!« Albert Munsel

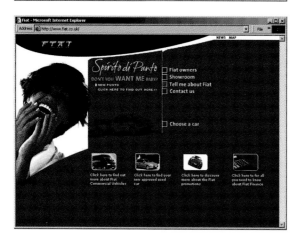

Trigger Emotions

We react very emotionally to images; that's why they can have such
a strong effect. Especially pictures
of people and pictures of situations
that trigger strong emotions (such
as the sunset) arouse feelings in us
whether we want this to happen or
not. Certainly previous experiences
and personal circumstances play an
important role here.

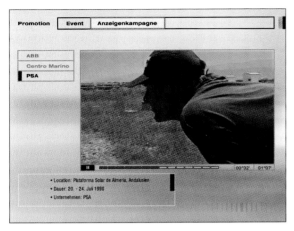

Create Depth
Give your image depth by working with foreground, middle ground, and background.

Generate Excitement
Generate excitement by placing your main motif deliberately. It is rarely a good idea to place the important motif in the middle of the image. Contrasts can also lend the image a certain dynamic force.

3.8 Icons

»People's reactions to icons are twofold: either they delight in clever helpful images, or they find them obscure enigmas, frustrating and pointless.« William Horton

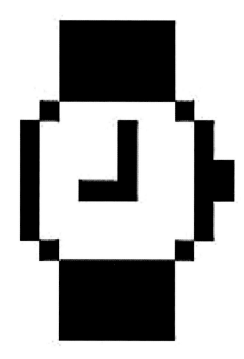

Symbolic, picture-like signs have existed in all cultures since the early days of mankind. Frequently these are signs that mark specific places (for example, a Gypsy's secret signs), that show the way, or that stand for specific objects. Familiar are the visual symbols on traffic signs, the pictographs on restrooms or in large buildings (exhibition halls, airports, railroad stations), and also the signs from the Middle Ages for the various trades.

This Chinese character on the left—also common in Japanese—means tree and wood. The Gypsy's secret signs shown on the right, frequently scratched inconspicuously on doorframes, stand for work (top) and dog (bottom).

Because of the dissemination of graphic user interfaces in recent years (such as Mac OS, GEM, Windows, OS/2 Warp, BeOS, KDE), the use of icons has become a matter of course.

One distinguishes generally two types of icons—icons that represent objects, and icons that represent functions.

The distinction between icon, ideogram, symbol, and pictograph is not always clear.

»**Ideograms** are signs that stand for an entire concept, that is, they are not so elementary as letters or numbers. They receive their meaning when a specific meaning is assigned permanently (coding) to a specific geometric figure. An additional distinguishing feature is that ideograms are of an abstract nature (ideo = Greek »idea«). Because there exists neither figurative similarity (such as with pictographs) nor a real relationship between an ideogram and its meaning, its interpretation must be learned.« (Charwat 1994, 219. The example shows the ideogram for a logic symbol.)

»**Pictographs** [...] are pictorial symbols that reproduce real objects or observable activities (such as participation in a particular type of sport) as stylized images. The sense of the word expressed in Latin also describes these circumstances, namely »pictus« = picture, and »graphum« = something written.« (Charwat 1994, 337. The example shows the pictograph for the sport of bicycling.)

»Basically, **symbol** stands for a picture or a word that says more than can be detected at first glance. It stands for a thing or a content. For example, the horn symbol stands for the German postal system.« (Charwat 1994, 421)

123

»Icons do not by themselves make a computer easier to use. Poorly designed or deployed icons may do just the opposite. … Icons do not make a product easier to use. Good design does.« William Horton

Icons are even more effective in combination with text. **Icons and text** should not exclude each other; rather, they should complement each another. Their great advantage lies precisely in their combination. For the inexperienced user of a product, most icons are just not recognizable intuitively. A description in key words—in the form of an explanatory balloon—is often helpful. For the advanced user, icons make the product a lot easier to use.

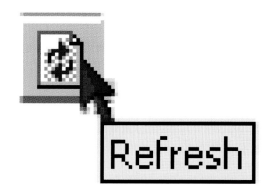

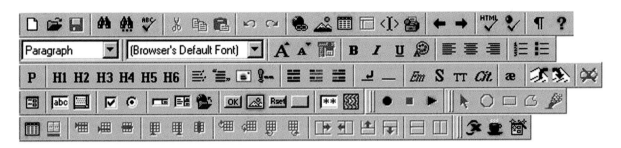

Use icons **sparingly** and selectively. Too many icons demand too much from the user and make the product difficult to use. Note here also the limits of human short-term memory that can hold and process approximately seven items simultaneously.

The example above shows the original user interface of an HTML editor. It has been changed in the meantime—why do you suppose that happened?

Group your icons on the screen. Provide this grouping with a spatial and logical order. In the example, the icons are grouped according to functionality. Here the user can recognize which icons belong together. In addition, the number of icons becomes visually clearer and easier to handle because of the grouping.

For software products, the arrangement of the icon bar at the top of the screen has become standard. Studies have shown that the upper area of the screen, in addition to the area at the left margin of the screen, is noticed more than the right margin or the bottom of the screen.

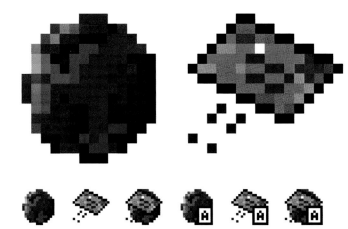

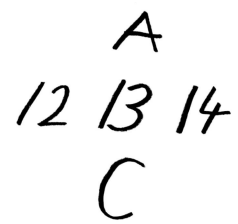

126

Note that icons are always interpreted by users. Among other things, the **context** in which the icons appear, for example, with other icons, influences the interpretation. The examples on the left show the icons of a mail program. The globe as an icon can mean just about anything. In combination with the »flying« envelope, its function becomes clearer. Can you guess the functionality that is hidden behind these six icons? (The answer is in the List of Illustrations and Sources in Appendix.)

The number-letter example to the left also illustrates a basic property of our perception—the inclusion of context. If you read the string of characters vertically, you interpret the middle character as the letter »B.« If you read the string horizontally, the same character means the number »13.«

In addition, the context of the user plays an essential role in the interpretation of an icon. Regular users of Microsoft Windows recognize the printer icon as the function »Print.« For those with little experience using Windows, however, the icon could stand for sending a fax or setting up a printer.

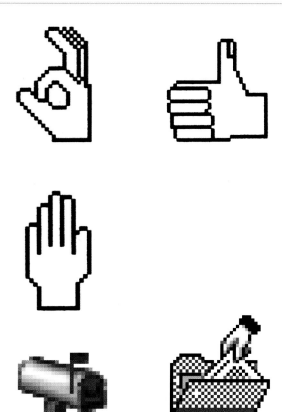

It is also important to know that icons can be interpreted differently by different cultures. All icons that represent hand gestures have a negative meaning in at least one **culture**. The open hand that is familiar to us as a warning or an indication to stop means a grave insult in the Arab culture (smearing camel excrement in the face). An outstretched finger also has an obscene meaning in some countries. In order to be safe, it is best to avoid using gestures as icons.

Mailboxes are not silver in every country and file folders do not always look like the icon represented to the left. If possible, test your icons with representatives of other cultures.

Icons should be **functional**, not beautiful. The point is not aesthetics; instead, the point is, the user should be able to recognize an icon or learn its meaning quickly. Icons should be reduced to that which is essential; they should not be used as decoration. In no case are they »small photos.« Any photo-realism only does damage. Use few colors and clear shapes. The efficiency of icons lies in their abstraction.

Compared to textual representation, icons have the following **advantages**:

- They require very little space.
- If they are familiar, they are recognized rapidly.
- They are language independent (but not culture independent).
- They are understandable to children and those who cannot read.
- They can be remembered easily if they are presented impressively.

Typical errors when presenting icons are as follows:

- Too many icons on the screen.
- Too few differences between the various icons.
- The icons are not combined into groups.
- The presentation is photo-realistic and not reduced to simple shapes.

Icons by Susan Kare

Designing Icons

The following procedure has proven to be successful:

1. Define the advantage and the purpose of the icon.
2. Describe the target group and, in so doing, take into consideration the previous knowledge and experience of the target group.
3. Collect ideas (with the help of brainstorming, mind maps, etc.).
4. Sketch the icon on paper.
5. Test the sketch(es) with the help of representatives of the target group by showing them the icon and asking its meaning or function.
6. Draw the icon with a suitable editor.
7. Run user tests again in which you check expectations, perception, and how easily the icon is learned.

3.9 Video, Animation, and Sound

Videos are pictures in motion. While pictures and text are time-independent media, videos (as well as animations, spoken text, or music) involve time-dependent media. This means that the order of events in a video (or an animation, or a sound clip) has a linear, chronological sequence. A video tells a story. In contrast to time-independent media, the user is tied to the order of events; he must view the video in a specific sequence. This is a certain constraint that contradicts the concept of interactive media and control by the user. For this reason, you should note the following things when using time-dependent media:

- Allow the user to control the video; give the user the capability to make a pause at any time, to stop the video, or to replay it.
- Keep in mind that where a multimedia product is concerned, you are not dealing with television. In contrast to TV, interactive media have an entirely different char-

acter and are used differently. Using a computer—in contrast to TV—involves a relatively active process. Accordingly, users also approach both media with very different expectations. For this reason, keep your time-dependent media short. Give the user the choice of watching the video or not, and indicate its duration so that the user knows how long he will be watching. Concentration diminishes quickly with videos on a PC. Short sequences up to 30 seconds are acceptable. Viewing longer than 1 minute becomes strenuous. If you have longer videos, enable the user to watch the video in short sections that are easy to grasp, or offer the user several short video sequences.

- To avoid the risk of users becoming impatient, you should always provide the possibility of skipping introductory videos because these videos become boring by the third time around.

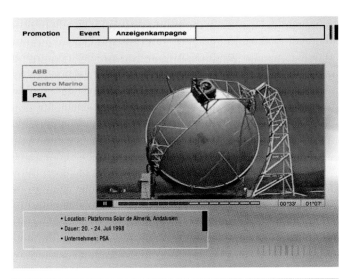

Control Elements

The information and control elements of a product CD-ROM of the Swiss office furniture company USM are exemplary. The unobtrusive line under the running video provides information on the length of the video (1 minute 7 seconds) and on the time that has already elapsed (33 seconds). The course of the video is also displayed by means of a progress indicator that provides a visual display indicating how much video has already been seen. In addition, the user can click on one of the segments of the indicator to jump to a certain position in the video film.

The example below from the *Encarta Encyclopedia* shows the control elements that are absolutely necessary for video, animation, and sound: Stop, Play (or Pause), Rewind, Fast Forward. These control elements help the user to watch the video sequence according to his wishes. Also consider a volume control.

131

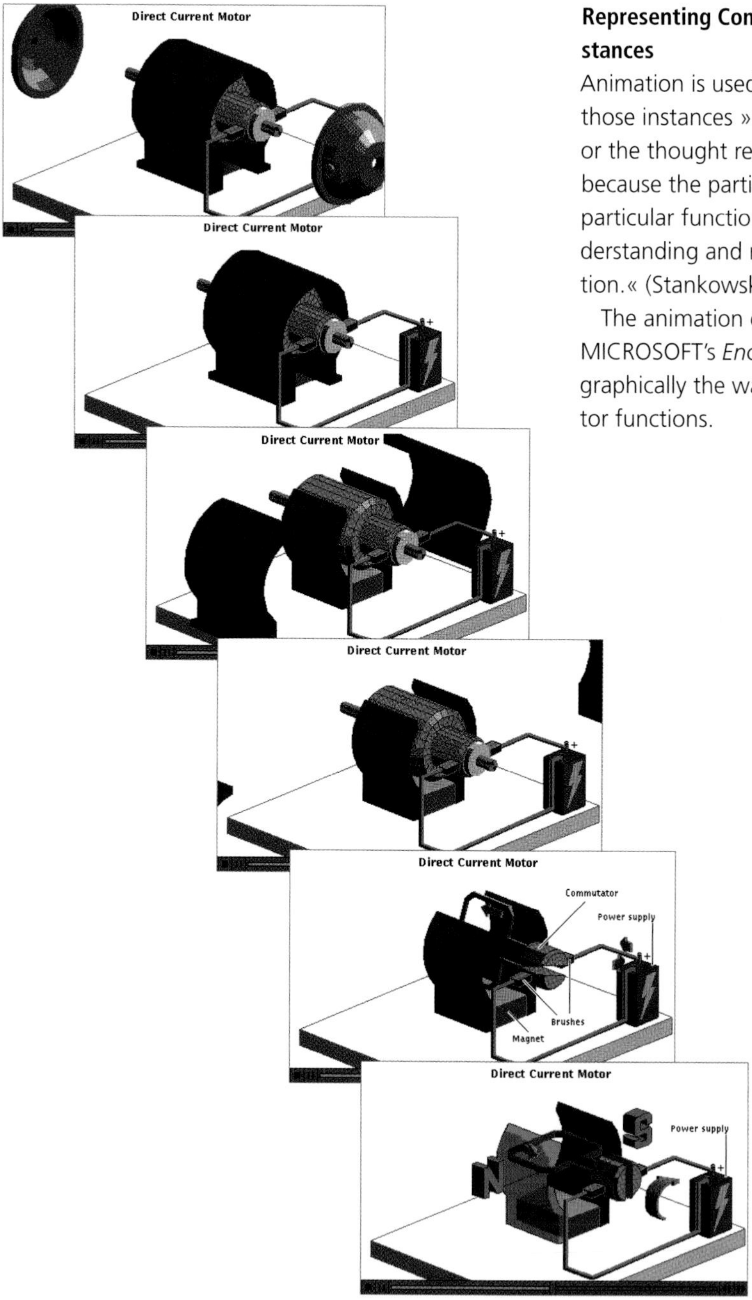

Direct Current Motor

Direct Current Motor

Direct Current Motor

Direct Current Motor

Direct Current Motor

Commutator
Power supply
Brushes
Magnet

Direct Current Motor

Power supply

Representing Complex Circumstances

Animation is used especially in those instances »where the word or the thought requires support because the particular topic or the particular function evades both understanding and naturalistic simulation.« (Stankowski 1994, 20)

The animation on the left from MICROSOFT's *Encarta 2000* explains graphically the way an electric motor functions.

»Users find this animation uniformly irritating. In fact, some users were so distracted by it that they could not even read the other text on the screen.« Spool et al. 1999

Be Careful with Animations for Their Own Sake

The quote shown above already illustrates the problem: blinking text, animated pictures, and everything that moves draws our attention.

However, this effect is so strong that it is difficult to avoid being trapped by it and to concentrate on the rest of the elements of the page. For this reason, use animation and motion very selectively and consciously. Otherwise you will make it difficult for the customer to use your product.

With blinking objects, note the following rules:

- Only one object should blink on the screen at a time.
- The length of time between the disappearance of the object and its reappearance should not be longer than half a second.
- The blink ratio for pictures should be 1:1 and for text approximately $1/_3$ to $2/_3$, that is, the text remains legible longer than it is invisible.
- Only individual words should blink, not several words or sentences.

Use of Spoken Text

What was said about video and animation also applies to spoken text: the user should be able to control and choose.

Use sound as a complement, not as competition. As a complement means as an accompaniment to an animation; as competition means displaying a text and reading it aloud at the same time. In most cases, this competition forces users to decide whether they should read the text or listen to the sound. In any case, use a professional speaker.

3.10 Flash

»We often overlook what's right in front of us. So, I have found that reminding even the most talented design teams of basic usability guidelines can result in substantially more usable sites and often time better looking sites.«
Tina Miletich, CEO of Girlzilla, Inc.

The Flash format of MACROME-DIA brought a lot of motion into the design of Web sites. Suddenly it was possible to combine videos, animation, sound, and interactive elements with each other and to achieve relatively grand effects with relatively small files. But this progress has its price: the user frequently requires a plug-in, that is, an additional program that he must install on his computer. In addition, the load times are too long for Internet access that is slow. And there is a very great danger of using Flash to design something beautiful and varied that may, however, not meet the requirements of the user, as the many annoying examples of Flash films show time and again.

Jakob Nielsen even sees the topic of Web usability being called into question, and in his first assessment, he comes to the conclusion: »Flash: 99% bad« (Nielsen 2000a).

Nielsen sees the use of Flash in the majority of Web sites as a **usability disaster**, because frequently Flash animations are used for their own sake. Because many Flash films offer little possibility to intervene, the user frequently loses control and the capability to interact—but these capabilities are exactly the basic principles of the WWW. In addition, every Flash animation contains its own Interface elements, and this situation forces the user to readapt to operating an animation again and again.

Other points of criticism by Nielsen are related to these lacking Interface standards: the Back button of the browser is disabled; the color of the links seldom conforms to the standard; the user does not have the capability to set the size of the text; it is difficult or impossible for handicapped users to operate Flash; and lastly, moving text

is harder to read than static text (Nielsen 2000a).

In spite of all the criticism of Flash, many of the bad examples that we find on the Internet are not a result of the capabilities of Flash, but of the fact that there were no standards previously and many creators of Flash animations did not bother much with usability.

Through the integration of standard interaction elements in the newest version of Flash (Flash MX) and the concentration of the Macromedia Company on the development of **ergonomic standards** as well as the advice of Flash developers, the situation has improved in the meantime. The following information points out the most important guidelines for an ergonomic Flash.

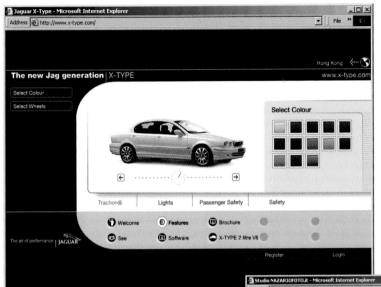

Flash shows its strength when the task at hand is to point out **complex relationships** or to develop something interactively. The site of the JAGUAR COMPANY makes this clear: the potential customers can configure their own X-Type model individually on the screen and examine the result immediately. Implementing this with HTML and JavaScript would be a very great effort.

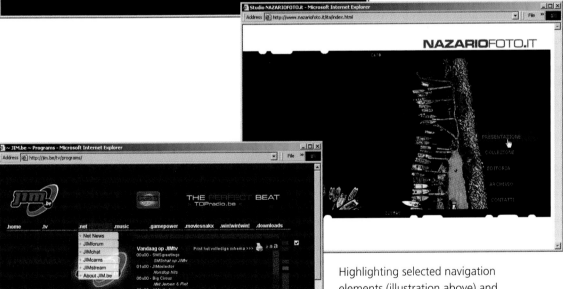

Highlighting selected navigation elements (illustration above) and displaying clear pull-down menus (illustration on the left) can be implemented very well with Flash. The price for this includes relatively long load times and the installation of a plug-in.

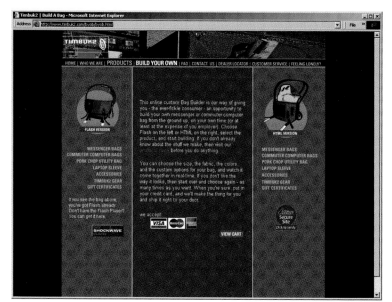

Keep in mind that there are still a lot of users who have very slow **access** to the Web. For this reason, always provide the HTML version in addition to the Flash site. Then the user has a choice and can decide to look at the Flash material or not.

Always visualize the course of a load procedure so that the user can estimate the amount of time it will take to call up the Flash film.

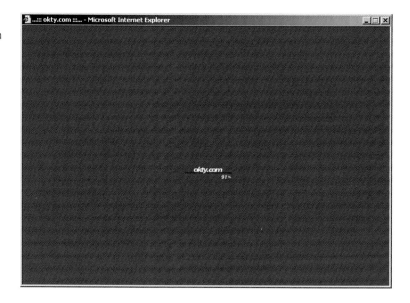

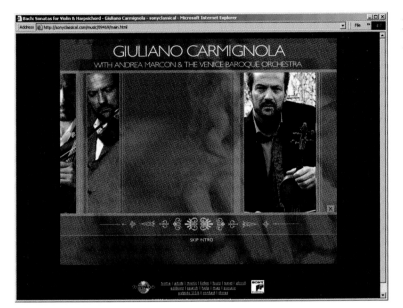

Avoid **unnecessary introductions**. They annoy the user, rob him of time and money (telephone charges), and are mostly superfluous. However, if an introduction is absolutely necessary, then give the user control over it, that is, allow the user to decide whether he wants to look at the introduction or not. And definitely provide the option of skipping the introduction.

- Use the familiar standard elements that are known to the Web users, such as scroll bars, buttons, and hot words.
- Always let the user know what the function of each element is. Also distinguish visually very clearly between elements for navigation, orientation, layout, and content.
- Integrate the use of the Back button of the browser, because the users are accustomed to this, and this capability to trace back the path in the Web is very popular and important.
- Apply animation appropriately. Animation should not be an end in itself; rather, it should reinforce your content and support the operation of the Web site.

3.11 Information Checklist

☐ Is your text prepared in a manner suitable to the screen?

☐ Do you distinguish between text to be read on the screen and text that the user will probably print out?

☐ Can the text that is to be read on the screen be scanned easily?

☐ Are the text passages subdivided into concise, meaningful sections? Can the content structure of your text also be clearly detected visually?

☐ Do you use the inverted pyramid style?

☐ Are the text passages concise and understandable? Do you use terms that are familiar to the users?

☐ Does your mode of expression fit your target group?

☐ Do you use clear titles that summarize your blocks of text concisely?

☐ Do you highlight key words visually?

☐ Do you use a sans serif font for your running text?

☐ Do you use typefaces (fonts) that are especially suited to the screen?

☐ Do you use the same, uniform font consistently for running text?

☐ Do you use a type size of at least 12 points?

☐ Do you use anti-aliasing?

☐ Do you avoid excessive use of boldface or italic type?

☐ Do you avoid underlining text (exception: links)?

- [ ] Do you avoid displaying text in all capital letters?

- [ ] Did you limit the line length (to 40–60 characters)?

- [ ] Do you use left-justified, ragged right text paragraphs?

- [ ] Do you use additional space (leading) between the paragraphs to distinguish them from each other clearly?

- [ ] Does the text stand out sufficiently from the background?

- [ ] Is the background sufficiently unobtrusive?

- [ ] Have you taken into consideration the use of colors and psychological and ergonomic factors?

- [ ] Can the scrolling of text be avoided?

- [ ] Which functions should the individual pictures that you used fulfill?

- [ ] Are the pictures focused on that which is essential?

- [ ] Does the use of figure titles appear appropriate to you?

- [ ] Do the pictures and text complement each other appropriately?

- [ ] Do your pictures communicate—or are they only decorations?

- [ ] Do you use conventional icons, that is, ones that are familiar to the target group?

- [ ] Do you use explanatory text (balloons) for the icons?

- [ ] Can the icons be distinguished clearly from other visual screen elements?

☐ Can the icons be distinguished clearly from each other? Are the icons differentiated enough?

☐ When using icons, did you take into consideration possible cultural peculiarities?

☐ Are the icons combined and grouped into units?

☐ Do you use no more than seven icons on each particular screen page?

☐ Do you use icons in the product consistently with regard to meaning and position?

☐ Are the icons easy to remember or learn?

☐ Do the time-dependent elements supplement the time-independent elements, or do they compete with each other?

☐ Can the user control videos, animation, and sound?

☐ Do you use the animations selectively and meaningfully?

☐ Have text passages been replaced with sound files?

☐ Do you use a professional spokesperson?

☐ What concrete advantages do your users have if you use Flash?

☐ What added value does the use of Flash bring to your users?

☐ Can the user always choose whether he wants to see your Flash films or not? Do you also provide pure HTML pages as an alternative?

- [ ] Do you explain to your users how they find and install a plug-in so that they can look at the Flash films?

- [ ] Do you explain to inexperienced users what the consequences are for them if they install the Flash plug-in?

- [ ] Can users skip the Flash animations (for example, introductions)?

- [ ] Are the load times of the Flash films still acceptable to users who have slow access to the Web?

- [ ] For your Flash animations, do you use standard elements that are familiar to the users?

- [ ] Can the users continue to employ the standard functions of the browser (such as the Back button)?

4 Screen Layout

This chapter deals with designing the screen so that its contents can be perceived as a unit. How should you place the individual elements? What do you need to keep in mind while doing this? How do people perceive visual arrangements? And how can you use the presentation of structures to clarify relationships?

4.1 Screen Layout as Composition

Selective Perception

Seeing is not a passive reception of optical information from the outside world; rather, it is an extremely active process of interpretation and evaluation of things which the eyes perceive. Of all the sense organs that handle the different types of perception, the eyes especially are extremely targeted and selective. We see those things that we expect and that we know and to which we direct our attention. We recognize a person for whom we are looking in a large crowd of people and overlook the new traffic sign on the everyday route to work. Because we are overwhelmed daily by a multitude of visual stimuli, our brain ignores the greater part of these stimuli and processes only those on which we concentrate consciously or those which receive a special, subjective significance based on our previous experience.

At the same time, we attempt to organize our perceptions and impressions permanently and unconsciously so that we can gain an overview and security. We categorize the world in our head and give all things a structure.

For the design of screen content, this means that users perceive and experience this content as a structured composition of different elements. A clear and well organized design facilitates »understanding« and access to the individual elements; a disorganized or overloaded structure requires a lot of cognitive effort composed of mental structuring of the things that are perceived. The design of a high quality multimedia product must always strike a balance: on the one hand, it has to be interesting to the user and therefore also must offer an appealing composition of elements; and on the other hand, the design must not demand too much of the user.

»Seeing is by no means only a mechanical recording of sensual impressions; rather, it proves to be a genuinely creative conception of reality–imaginative, ingenious, clever, and beautiful. [...] All perception is also thinking, all thinking is also intuition, all observation is also invention.«
Rudolf Arnheim

Conception

Before developing your product, create a concept for the design of your screen pages. In so doing, note the following points:

- When designing the screen, perceive its content as a unit—the user does this also. Compose the displayed elements, that is, have them appear in relationship and as complements to each other.
- Be consistent. In this manner, you will enable the user to experience your product as a harmonious whole.

- Decide according to each target group how structured or how frivolous your screen composition should be. Don't bore the user, but don't demand too much of the user either through the arrangement of screen elements.

»Above all in the design, the following saying applies: less is more.«
Ralf Brugger

The three basic principles of visual communication according to Aaron Marcus:

1. The **organization principle**: »Give the user a simple, clear, and consistent conceptual structure.«
2. The **economic principle**: »Maximize the effectivity of a minimal set of resources.«
3. The **communication principle**: »Adapt your presentation to the user's capacity to comprehend.«

4.2 Scanning a Picture

»Seeing means comprehending a few prominent features of objects.«
Rudolf Arnheim

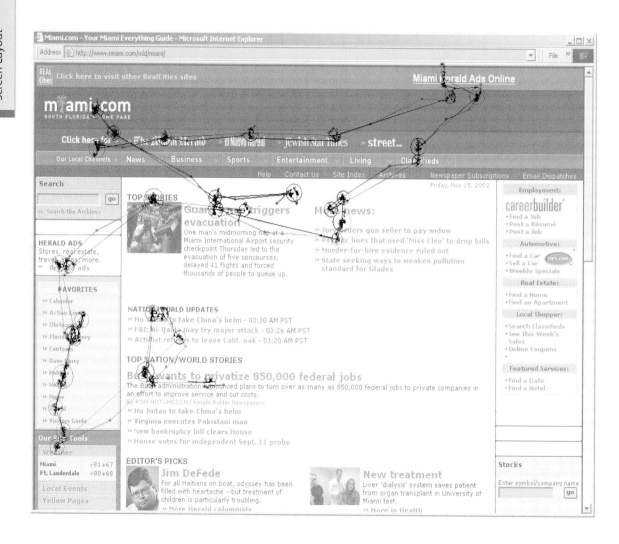

When we direct our attention to a picture, initially our eyes skim the picture and scan it superficially for prominent features.

In this manner, the brain gets an orientation to the total context.

In a second step, we view the prominent features more exactly and more intensively. The details do not follow until afterward. The more **structure** the screen composition establishes, the simpler the comprehension.

The more unstructured the screen is, the more the eye must seek, the more energy the brain must expend to define a structure, and the more unwilling the user becomes to work with the picture.

The illustrations on these two pages show a »screen scan« of different Web pages taken with a vision registration camera.

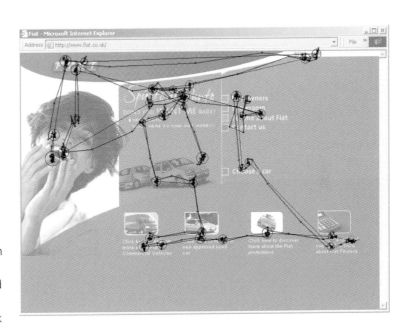

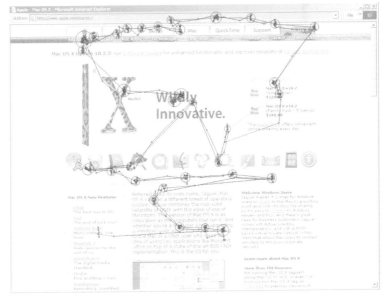

4.3 Structuring the Content of the Screen

An implicit structure of the screen contents establishes a relationship among the individual elements and thus allows them to become a whole. The examples of these pages show a few »design grids« of various screen pages.

For the creator of multimedia products, it is recommended to draft basic patterns for the structure of screen pages. Initially, determine which elements you need and then define their arrangement. While doing this, think about shapes, spatial areas, and the course of lines before you go into detail.

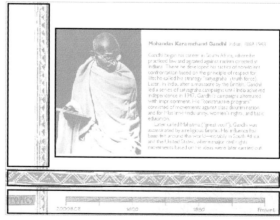

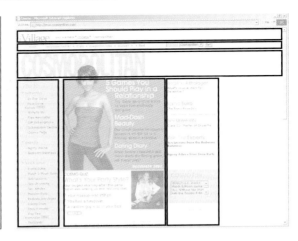

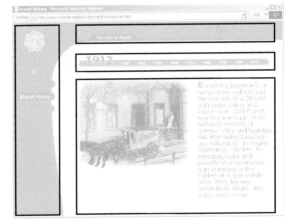

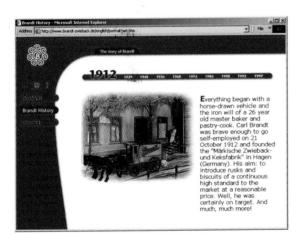

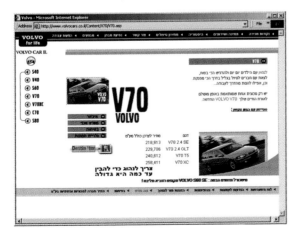

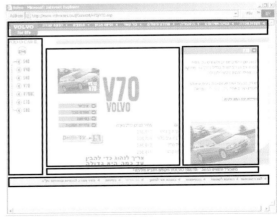

4.4 Figure-Ground Relationship

The **background** on which the various elements lie serves as a framework and **visual stopping point**. Often used throughout the entire multimedia product (or throughout individual thematic areas), the background lends the product a certain consistency. The background often visualizes the topic and sets up a suitable atmosphere whose context reinforces the actual meaning of the information elements. It emphasizes the elements of the screen page visually.

So the background plays an important role. Of course, it must not be too dominant; otherwise, it disturbs the picture and destroys its harmonious totality.

Psychologists call the differentiation of objects from their background **figure-ground relationship**.

When we fixate our eyes on objects in the world, we focus our gaze, perceive the remaining field of vision imprecisely, and simply note this remaining field unconsciously. The total sharpness of all the objects in the room would overwhelm us and result in an overflow of stimuli that we could not process. The illustration that shows a vase or two faces provides an example of this. Try to see both—faces and vase—at the same time. You won't be able to do it.

The problem that we have when elements and background cannot be differentiated clearly enough is illustrated by the two pictures on the left.

It takes a bit of effort to become oriented. In the example of the chaotic desk, the user is confused on purpose and his drive for discovery is challenged. First he must look around in order to recognize what is actually involved and which elements he can activate by clicking on them.

On the French Web site of the COCA COLA COMPANY, the dominance of the background is so reduced by an intense brightness and haziness that all that is left of the background visually is the mere suggestion of a context.

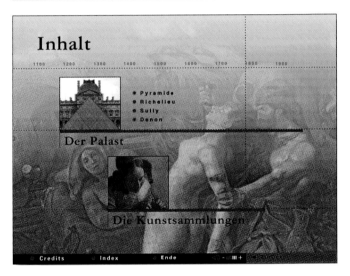

An information CD about the LOUVRE in Paris uses the background intensively to represent a particular epoch with the help of a typical painting.

Here, too, a mild haziness and brightening reduce the dominance of the background.

Rules for the Effective Use of Background

- The background should present a thematic and visual framework that the user can understand.
- It should never dominate, for then it would distract from the foreground and destroy the harmonious interplay of the individual elements in the foreground.
- A small object in front of a larger background is perceived more readily as a figure than a large object is in front of a smaller background. For this reason, work with large areas and few (bright) colors in your background. Haziness is an additional means of allowing the background to recede.

4.5 Gestalt Laws and Their Application

What Are Gestalt Laws?

At the beginning of the 20th century, a few psychologists (including Koffka, Köhler, Wertheimer, and Arnheim) described patterns of human perception in the so-called »Gestalt laws.«

They understood these Gestalt laws as principles that have universal validity. Taking note of these laws will help us in composing the elements of a screen so that these elements suit human perception. The following pages provide a sketch of the most important Gestalt laws.

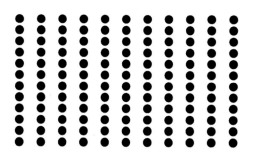

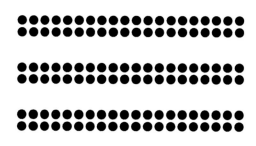

The Law of Proximity

Elements that are close to each other spatially are perceived as belonging together. On the left, you see columns of dots; on the right, you probably see rows.

Consequence: Group the elements that belong together close to each other.

The law of proximity is used in the directory page of GOOGLE. The different areas are separated from each other by spatial intervals.

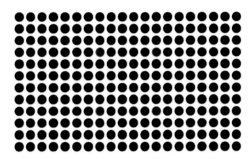

The Law of Similarity

Elements that look like each other are perceived by human cognition as belonging together. In the example, you see four red dots in the form of a square. It appears to be indisputable that they belong together.

Consequence: Mark elements that belong together so that they are similar visually.

The law of similarity is used on the Web site of the AMAZON book dealer: the similarly displayed elements belong together functionally.

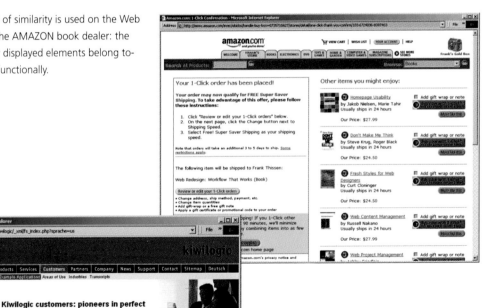

153

With KIWILOGIC, similarity (orange colored areas) signals shared identity in functionality: the upper and left areas are used for navigation and interaction, while the beige area contains the information.

The Law of Symmetry

Elements that are arranged symmetrically to each other are interpreted as a unit. Symmetrical and asymmetrical structures are perceived such that the symmetrical ones are ascribed to the figure (foreground) and the asymmetrical ones are related to the background.

Consequence: Symmetrical arrangements create strong structures; asymmetrical arrangements cause the elements to be lost on the screen.

The image structure of the Apollinaris page has a symmetrical division; in this manner, the screen content has a clear structure and is subdivided into a navigation area and an information area.

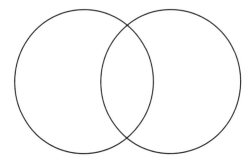

The Law of Good Continuity

Visual elements that are arranged in a certain continuity (for example, along a line) are perceived as belonging together. In the example, you see two intersecting circles, not two disks with portions cut out of them.

Consequence: Arrange elements that belong together along a line.

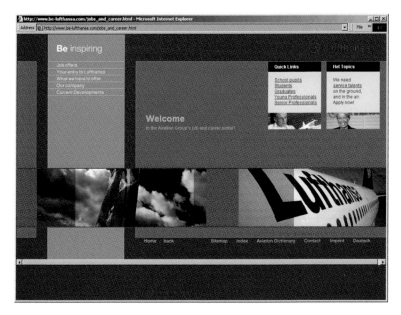

The example of the LUFTHANSA site illustrates the law of good continuity: on the page you see three pastel colored rectangles above which a bar with images is located; not three rectangles above, the bar, and under that three additional rectangles.

The Law of Simplicity

Visual perception tends toward a simple and consistent organization of elements. Simple and self-contained structures stand out better from their background.

Consequence: In your presentation of screen elements, provide structures that are as simple as possible; in this manner, you facilitate concentration on the actual contents.

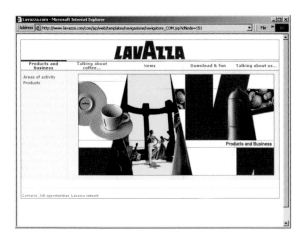

The example from NESTLE shows distinctive and clear shapes and areas. This presentation facilitates comprehension of the screen page and visual orientation. With the example above (LAVAZZA), the viewer is more likely to have difficulties.

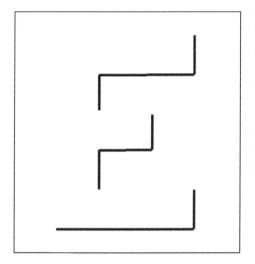

The Law of Experience

Visual perception always goes back to already existing experiences and automatically completes patterns that are incomplete. In the example, you see the letter »E« because this letter is familiar to you.

Consequence: You don't always have to show everything; rather, you can incorporate the previous experiences and previous knowledge of your target group.

The law of experience is used with many images. If your perception would not automatically complete the things that you see, you would not see a dog's face on the left; rather, you would see a dog's face cut in two.

157

4.6 Controlling Eye Movement by Means of Visual Signals

Good screen pages are not dull; rather, they convey a certain excitement and dynamic force. Quiet areas should be located opposite to those areas in which something is happening, that push themselves into the foreground. Only from this combination can you design exciting pages. You should also make a visual distinction between important things and unimportant things. How do you implement that? By using warm signal colors, »powerful« images, highlighted headings, strong contrasts, and page division that distinguishes quiet places from »lively« pages.

The examples on this page show how you can design this excitement.

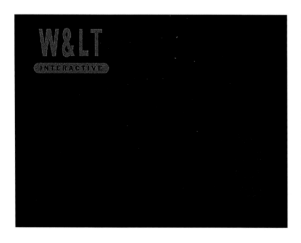

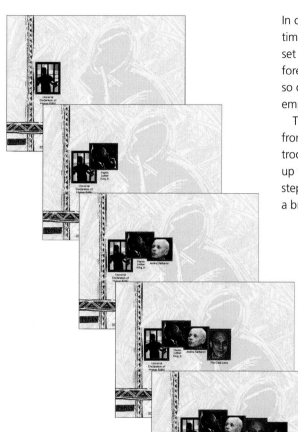

In contrast to printed media, multimedia gives you the capability to set up the screen step-by-step before the eyes of the viewer and, in so doing, to clarify a structure and emphasize important material.

The CD-ROM on human rights from AMNESTY INTERNATIONAL introduces the main topics by setting up the navigation elements step-by-step while a spokesperson provides a brief introduction to each topic.

4.7 Colors

Using colors enables you to add another dimension to your information. Colors suggest their own message subliminally, trigger feelings, and can support your assertions or falsify them. They can help with orientation, structure information, and clarify differences. But they can also facilitate access to information. Frequently, colors are perceived unconsciously, and they always trigger emotions.

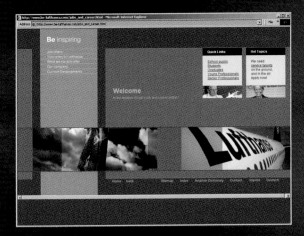

There are three influences on our subjective perception of color:

1. Biological Bases

Based on our system of perception, we perceive the color red, for example, considerably more intensively than the color blue. This phenomenon is also related to the fact that we have considerably more sensory cells for the colors red (approximately 64%) and green (approximately 34%) on the retina of our eyes than for the color blue (approximately 2%). In nature there are only a very few things that are really red. Among them is the glow of a fire or blood. In the example on the left, the signal color red draws attention to the image.

2. Cultural Bases

Our perception of colors is strongly influenced by culture. An extreme example of this is the perception of the color black: while in the Western culture this color embodies death and evil, among other things, in Egypt it stands for rebirth and resurrection; and in the Hebrew culture it means understanding. Even the corporate design of a company is frequently distinguished by a specific color or color combination. The example on the left shows the recurring color combination white-gray-orange on the Web site of the German airline Lufthansa.

3. Individual Bases

Finally, all of us have our preferences and aversions for special colors, and these likes and dislikes can even change over time. Fashions also have a great influence on our taste. For example, the color orange was very popular in the 1970s, then was hardly used for a long time, and now is experiencing a renaissance. The »plastic green« in the example is also such a fashion color.

You should keep these types of perception in mind when designing your product. Consider the color perception that distinguishes your target group and what you want to convey with the colors that you choose. Use colors selectively to underscore your message.

4.8 Color Systems

Hue 23:
Left: Saturation 100% / lightness 0%, 25%, 50%, 75%
Right: Lightness 50% / saturation 100%, 75%, 50%, 25%

The HLS Color Space

Colors are described by means of the model of the so-called color space. One distinguishes generally three types of color perception:

1. Hue

The hue reproduces the actual color property (gradation) of a color. It is defined in steps of 360°, whereby red corresponds to 0°, yellow to 60°, green to 120°, cyan to 180°, blue to 240°, and magenta to 300°.

2. Lightness

Color lightness reproduces the perception of light intensity, the illumination of a color. It is defined in percentages from 0 to 100%.

100% color lightness generates the color white, 0% lightness generates the color black. 50% lightness corresponds to the pure hue. Colors with a high lightness have a light effect; those with little lightness have a heavy effect.

3. Saturation

Color saturation reproduces the purity and unadulterated quality of a color and defines its gray portion. It is defined in percentages from 0 to 100%. A color with high saturation (100% = no gray portion) reproduces the particular hue; an unsaturated color (0%) is gray (= highest portion of gray).

Highly saturated colors have a heavy effect and often push themselves into the foreground. »Pure« colors are rare in nature. Less saturated colors have a more unobtrusive effect and are better used as background colors.

The RGB Color Space

The various colors on the screen are formed by means of three electron beams that are emitted toward a pane of glass that is coated with phosphor.

This action creates a grid that is composed of the three basic colors **red, green, and blue** (RGB). Mixed colors arise from the varying intensity of the three basic colors. Because each of the three colors can take on an intensity of 256 levels, the result (256 x 256 x 256) is approximately 16 million displayable colors.

When all three colors illuminate with their highest intensity, together they generate the color white. On the other hand, if they illuminate with their lowest intensity, they produce the color black. Here one refers to **additive mixing of colors**, as opposed to the **subtractive mixing of colors**, which is applied in the **CMYK model** (cyan-magenta-yellow-black) for printing. The colors of the additive color mixing are called light colors; those of the subtractive color mixing are called pigment colors.

Note when designing your products that you can never determine exactly how the colors will appear on the particular monitor of the observer because the following factors influence the display:

- Setting of the color depth (a few of the older graphics cards can display only 256 colors)
- Setting of the brightness and contrast of the particular monitor
- Gamma setting and color calibration of the monitor
- Computer system and operating system (Apple computers display colors more brightly than Windows systems)
- Web browser for Internet pages

4.9 The Use of Color

»Above all, do not harm.« Edward Tufte

There have been countless attempts to classify colors. One of these is the **color circle** according to Johannes Itten (Swiss painter and graphic artist, 1888–1967), who arranged the three primary pigment colors yellow, magenta red, and cyan blue, each with their intermediate stages.

The combination of related colors, that is to say, the ones close to each other (such as blue and green), has a restful and well-balanced effect. The combination of complementary colors (such as blue and red) brings excitement and has a vivacious effect.

The colors in the upper part of the color circle are also designated as cool colors, while those of the lower part are called warm colors. Cool colors are perceived spatially as somewhat recessed, while warm colors press into the foreground. The more saturated a color is, the more dominant its effect.

The use of a limited number of colors (two or three) that go well with each other is recommended for normal applications. Very few users accept an abundance of harsh, glaring colors; such a combination results in a restless total picture and confuses most users. Use colors consistently.

It is easy to emphasize something on un-

obtrusive colors.

On glaring colors, it is difficult to empha-

size something.

So-called cold colors have an unobtrusive and low-key effect. They are very suitable as background colors and provide a quiet and unobtrusive framework.

The dark green of the Web site of a natural cosmetics business signals freshness and naturalness. The text is easily readable on the dark hue.

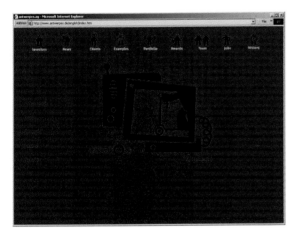

Warm colors have a cheerful and activating effect. However, they are quite dominant and »loud.« For this reason, you should use them very selectively.

The ANTWERPES ADVERTISING AGENCY signals liveliness and vitality on its pages by means of an orange background. The black graphics go very well with the background, for color illustrations or multicolor navigation elements would have a hard time because of the dominant orange.

The combination of cold blue and a warm yellow allow the build up of excitement here. Blue stands for technology and reliability; yellow gives the page something warm and friendly. Two warm colors or two cold ones are more likely to compete with each other.

An advertising CD of the W.&.L.T. Company that provides fireworks of color shows that the color green can be very dominant by means of a touch of yellow. The slogan »kiss the future« and the extravagant fashion of the posh brand are presented here fittingly. Everything on this CD cries out, is bubbling over with vividness and modernity. It is exactly this that appeals to the target group.

In general, unsaturated pastel colors have the advantage of having a reserved yet friendly effect. Colorful markings can then be highlighted well on them, as the letter »M« makes clear in the example below.

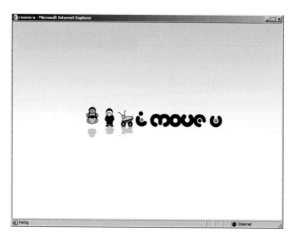

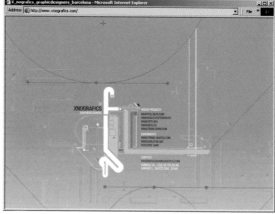

The Internet material of the Stuttgart Zoo—WILHELMA—changes its background color according to season. In this way, the user receives the signal that the things the zoo has to offer apply not only to the warm part of the year, but that a visit in winter can also be attractive.

Red

Activity
Dynamic force
Energy
Determination

Life
Vitality
Solidity

Love
Sensuality
Sexuality
Pleasure
Desire
Passion
Temptation

Power
Vivacity
Impulsiveness

Fire
Heat
Danger
Warning

Aggressiveness
Hate
Anger

Red is the strongest and most dominating of all colors. It is full of vivacity and mobilizes its observers. Often it is associated with blood and fire, but also with love, sensuality, and passion. In Europe, it was the color of the nobility because crimson was obtained from the rare and expensive kermes lice.

In Russia at the beginning of the 20th century, it was the color of the revolution. It is the color of the workers' movement and of communism.

Red stands for both life and danger. Red is the signal color par excellence and thereby achieves increased attention. Stop signs are red, and so are warning notices.

In China, red signifies luck and joy; in Hinduism the color stands for creativity and activity and is worn as a favorite color at weddings. In Japan, red is the color of the rising sun, but it also stands for rage and danger. In Islamic countries, red has a rather negative significance, such as in Egypt, where red is the color of evil and destruction.

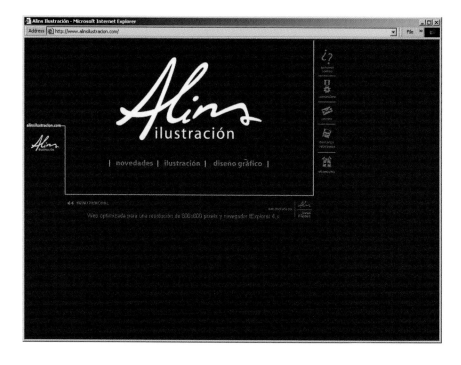

Orange

Warmth
Liveliness
Exuberance
Wildness
Energy

Activity
Attention
Courage
Obtrusiveness

Sociability
Fun
Happiness
Enjoyment

Artificiality
Safety

Orange is a very lively and cheerful color. It signals unconventionality, dynamic force, and exuberance.

It made its triumphal advance in connection with the
development and widespread dissemination of modern
plastics in the 1970s and for this reason is often still
associated with cheap plastic. In Europe, orange is the
most unpopular color after brown.

It signals both safety and orderliness (orange trash-
cans, the orange clothing of street cleaners, safety col-
or in factories) as well as sociability (the warm glow of
the light bulbs in a restaurant in the evening).

Orange is the color of Buddhism. In Japan and China
it stands for love and happiness, and in the Hebraic culture it is the color of splendor.

Orange also stands for creativity and extravagance.

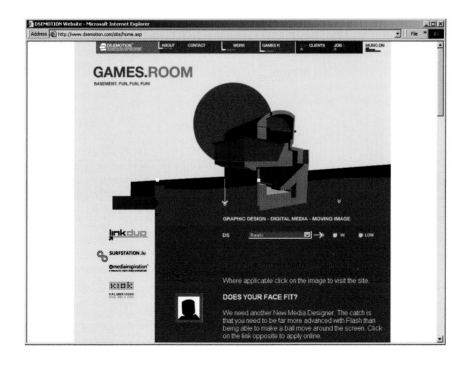

Yellow

Sun
Warmth
Brightness

Cheerfulness
Liveliness
Frivolity
Happiness

Optimism
Friendliness
Sense of honor

Value
Gold
Royalty

Jealousy
Envy
Malevolence
Annoyance

Cowardice
Untruthfulness
Stinginess
Egotism
Obtrusiveness
Social devaluation

Yellow stands for sunshine, warmth, and comfort. It is the color of gold and of prosperity. Foods that are yellow are perceived as appetizing, for example, golden-yellow egg noodles or bright yellow egg yolks. Yellow is also the color of refreshment, of the sour and the bitter — one only has to think of the lemon.

Historically, however, time and again yellow was the color of those who were ostracized, such as prostitutes and heretics in the Middle Ages and of the Jews who were subjected to discrimination in Europe since the 12th century.

For the American Indians, yellow stands for death; in China, on the other hand, it is the color of the emperors. In the Hebraic culture, yellow stands for beauty, and in Japan, it stands for charm and grace. Generally, yellow is the color of Asia for many Europeans. In the Middle East, yellow symbolizes joy and prosperity.

Green

Nature
Vegetation
Growth
Opulence
Freshness
Health
Youth

Peace and quiet
Balance
Relaxation
Recuperation

Peacefulness
Security
Hope

Poison
Bitterness
Sourness

Green is the color of nature, of freshness, and of life. Green embodies spring and stands for hope. Green embodies stability, rest, and peacefulness; it has a relaxing and comforting effect.

At the same time, green is the color of things that are poisonous and inedible. As copper verdigris, it is extremely hazardous to one's health.

The American Indians associate green with peace; in Christianity, green is the color of the Holy Spirit; and in Islam, green is the color of the Prophet and thereby of the religion. The Chinese associate fertility with this color, and the Irish have green as their national color. For the Buddhists, green is the color of life, and for the Hebraic culture, it is the color of victory.

In France, however, green is an unlucky color; for this reason, green cars are very unpopular there. And the Hindus consider green as the color of death.

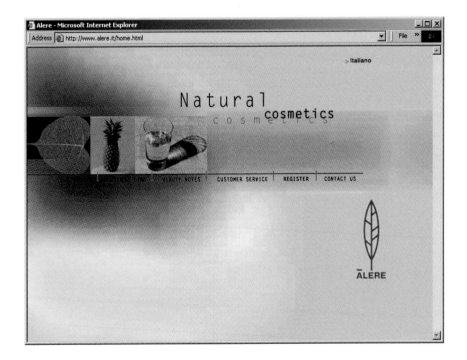

Blue

Expanse
Depth
Infinity
Eternity
Yearning

Tranquility
Harmony
Intuition
Balance

Spirit
Credibility
Faithfulness
Trust
Friendliness
Friendship

Achievement
Seriousness
Sympathy

Masculinity
Sportsmanship

Coolness
Passiveness
Lack of motion

Blue is the color of expanse, of the sky, and of eternity. It has the effect of reserved elegance. In front of sober blue, warm colors—preferably the complementary color orange—stand out with extreme intensity.

It is claimed that most people name blue as their favorite color. In any case, the color is extremely popular. It possesses something noble, stable, amicable, likable. It is a masculine color that is also used widely in the world of sports.

However, blue also stands for sobriety, for logic and sharp thinking, as well as for technology.

Blue is the color associated with laborers, in contrast to the »white-collar workers« in offices.

Blue rooms have a cool or even cold effect.

For the Japanese, blue is the color of scoundrels and villains. For the Buddhists, blue stands for coolness and wisdom; in the Middle East, it stands for fidelity and truth. In almost all religions, blue is the divine color, the color of the sky.

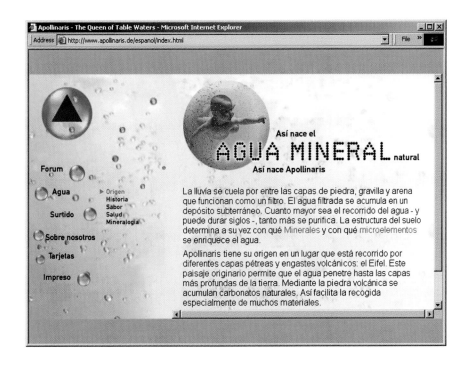

Purple

Dominion
Power

Sacredness
Piety
Nostalgia

Magic
Seclusion

Self-centeredness
Vanity
Decadence

Extravagance
Unconventionality

Loneliness
Contentedness
Grief
Passion
Humility

Feminism

Purple is the color of power and dominion. In the Roman Empire, only the emperor was allowed to wear this color. This custom was maintained in the Middle Ages, but with the addition of bishops dressed in purple. In this way, it became the color of the church and in Christianity it took on the symbolism of penance, humility, and passion.

Purple is also the color of magic and esotericism, of the obscure and the secret.

Around 1900, art nouveau prized purple as a room color and preferred it in clothing. Simultaneously, it became the color of decadence.

As a compound color between the sexes (red = feminine, blue = masculine), purple became the color of the feminist movement in the 1970s.

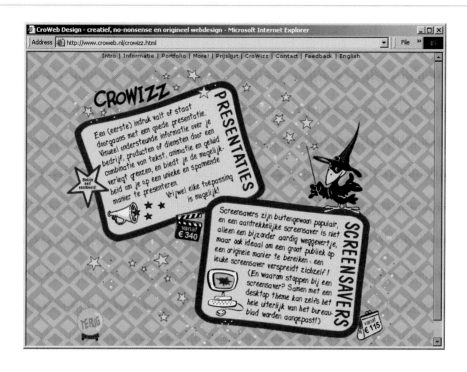

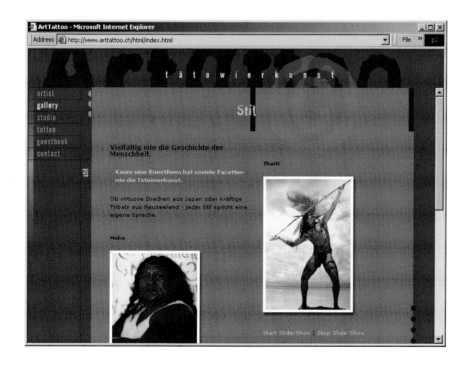

Pink

Delicate
Soft
Gentle
Sensitive

Baby
Delightful
Naive
Mild

Feminine
Charm
Polite

Vain

Tender
Romance
Sweet

Pink is the color of affection and tenderness. Babies are dressed in pink clothes, but pink is also the color of young ladies and stands for charm, friendliness, and youth.

Pink calls to mind roses, fragrances, sweets, and candy. There is always something sweet about pink.

For a number of years now, pink has also become the color of homosexuals. In more recent times, pink has experienced a toning down of its significance, to the extent that a large German telephone company uses the color pink (strictly speaking, magenta) as the color of its corporate design.

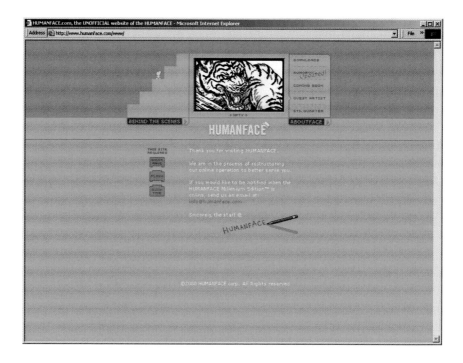

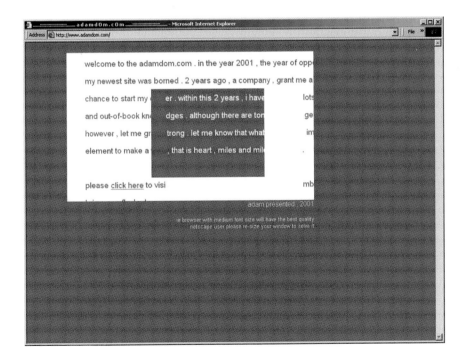

Brown

Indigenous
Earthy
Close to nature

Aromatic

Old-fashioned
Enduring
Well-adjusted
Simple
Commonplace
Cozy
Boring
Mediocre

Stupid
Lazy
Unappealing

Autumn
Transitory
Spoiled

In Western culture, brown is obviously the most unappealing color of all. Although this color plays a large role with furniture (wood paneling) and clothing (trousers, sweaters, shoes), surveys indicate that people frequently express their dislike for this color.

Brown is the color of filth, of excrement. It is reminiscent of the loamy earth, but also of the withered leaves in autumn—it is the patina of the ephemeral.

Brown reminds us of antiques; it stands for the past, the old-fashioned, and things that are simple.

Brown takes on a somewhat more positive meaning as the color of *Gemütlichkeit*, the color of wood, leather, and unbleached wool. Coffee is brown and aromatic; brown bread is crispy.

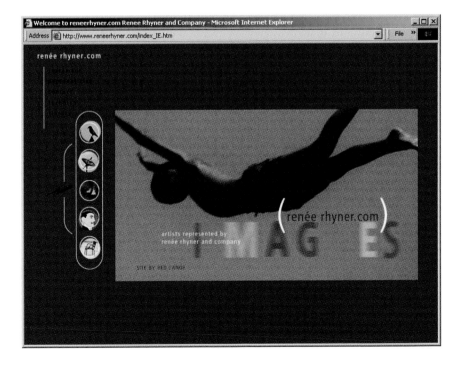

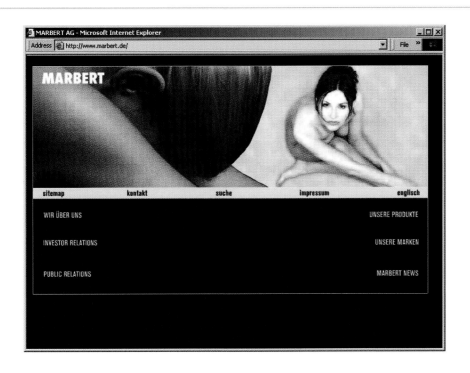

Black

Elegant
Dignified
Heavy
Powerful

Night
Lonely
Empty

Secret
Forbidden
Impenetrable
Magical

Evil
Brutal
Hard
Unfriendly
Negation

Conservative

Death
Mourning
Melancholy
Egotism

In Western culture, black is the color of death and mourning. It also stands for negative feelings, for misfortune, darkness, and night. Things which are forbidden are often black, for example »blackleg« (American »scab«) with reference to union workers, or »black magic«. Black is also the color of pirates and anarchists.

As the color of the Protestant robes in the Reformation, black contrasted with the colorfulness of Catholicism and in this way took on a certain severity and soberness.

Since the 1970s, black has become a popular fashion color that is intended to express cool elegance and dignity. In the technical field, black is often the preferred color for high-tech products such as photo cameras and stereo equipment.

In Africa, black is the most beautiful color and represents the people in the flags and coats of arms of African states. Black is the color of the fertile earth and as such is the color of prosperity.

In Buddhism, black is the color of oppression. In China, black stands for the yin and symbolizes winter and water. The Egyptians see black as representing rebirth and resurrection. The Hebrews associate understanding and comprehension with black. And for Hindus, black is the color of decline.

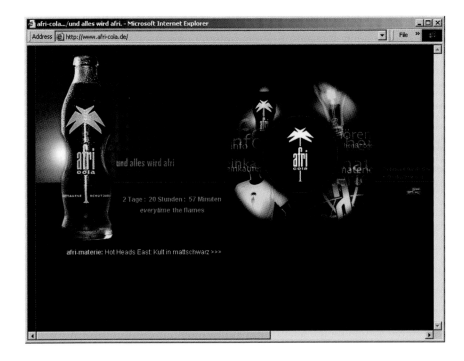

Hasselblad Website - Microsoft Internet Explorer

Address http://www.hasselblad.com/

HASSELBLAD

NEWS
PRODUCTS
ADDRESSES
THE COMPANY
IMAGE GALLERY
ARTICLES
LINKS TO:

XPAN
www.xpan.com

New!
905swc

Now
in colour!

HASSELBLAD USA   HASSELBLAD HK

Mail to Hasselblad [info@hasselblad.se]

bauhaus-archiv museum of design - Microsoft Internet Explorer

Address http://www.bauhaus.de/english/index.htm

bαuhαus-αrchiv museum of design

klingelhöferstrasse 14 • 10785 berlin • germany • telephone 0049 - 030 - 254 00 20   deutsch

bauhaus-archiv   building   museum   collections   bauhaus 1919-33   news   information   bauhaus shop

made by marketing factory   imprint

Gray

Neutral
Sober

Theory
Pensive

Elegant
Objective
Technology

Boring
Conformist
Unassuming
Mediocre
Insecure

Lonely
Secret
Unfriendly

Old

Hopeless
Miserable
Insensitive

Gray is the color between black and white—the average, without character. Gray is the color of neutrality and the insignificant (a »gray mouse« is a woman who is not very noticeable).

Gray also stands for November, gloomy weather, and depression. Gray is the color of age and of the past.

The »gray eminence« is the concealed person pulling the strings behind the scenes. The world of spirits is gray—and the fog.

However, gray can also signal elegance. The gray suit, the gray blouse, the gray background on which bright colors can shine in high contrast. Objectivity and neutrality are also often associated with gray. However, using gray runs the risk that the color becomes boring.

A few Indian tribes in North America find gray beautiful and cheerful, probably because the gray rain clouds are extremely welcome to them. For the Hebrews, gray is the color of wisdom.

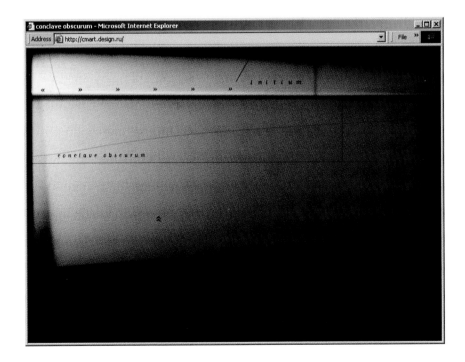

White

Pure
Clean
Innocent
Clear
Lightweight
Orderly

Neutral
Objective
New
Modern

Good
Ideal

Functional

Perfect
Authentic
Honest
True

Pious

Softly

In Western culture, white is the color of purity and cleanliness. It is the color of clarity, of objectivity, and of things that are unadulterated. White embodies innocence. Physicians wear white, but so do bakers.

However, white is also the color of the dead (white shroud) and of ghosts (the »white lady« in gothic novels).

In many religions, white stands for godliness, light, and purity. Hindu priests like to dress in white. The American Indians associate white with birth and life.

In Asia, white is the color of mourning that is worn for burials. In Japan, white stands for death and mourning.

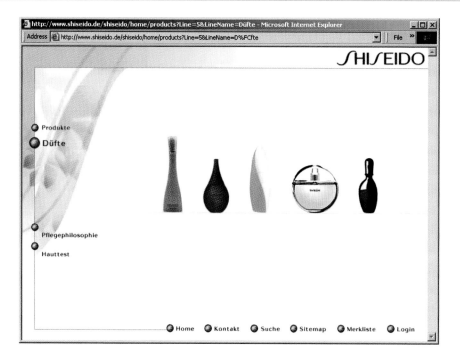

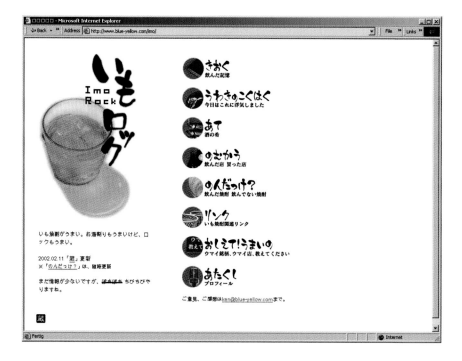

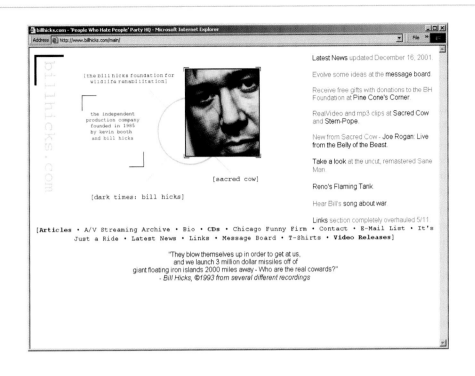

4.10 Screen Layout Checklist

☐ Have you defined one or more »design grids« for your product that specify how the elements on the screen should be arranged?

☐ Are the various screen pages similar in structure?

☐ Should different thematic areas be structured differently?

☐ Do you provide support for the user to find his way around with the help of a clear arrangement of the screen contents?

☐ Is the screen »overloaded?«

☐ Is there enough »breathing room« around the screen elements?

☐ Are the individual elements of the screen page clearly recognizable and can they be distinguished from each other?

☐ Are navigation, orientation, and content elements separated from each other visually or are they supposed to be interwoven?

☐ Have you organized the visual elements »logically« and is this arrangement understandable to the user?

☐ Are functionally similar elements also displayed consistently, according to clear, straightforward rules?

☐ When arranging your elements, did you take into consideration the findings of Gestalt psychology (»Gestalt laws«)?

☐ Did you group related elements together?

- ☐ Is the background not too dominant (figure-ground relationship)?

- ☐ Does the background fit the topic?

- ☐ In what manner do you *guide* the user during visual disclosure of the screen?

- ☐ Are the screen pages constructed step-by-step or do they appear all at once?

- ☐ How are colors used? To emphasize something, to motivate, to serve as a setting for the topic?

- ☐ What associations will the target group probably make with the colors that you used?

- ☐ Are you taking into consideration the biological, cultural, and individual color perceptions of the target group?

- ☐ How do the colors that you used support the message(s) of your product?

5 Interaction

Interaction is an essential element in multimedia systems. It enables the computer to react to the actions of the user. What does a screen designer need to keep in mind when using interactive elements? What are the boundaries of interactivity? Where does it help, where does it hinder?

5.1 Interaction as a Human Basic Constant

Interaction is a basic constant of human communication. With every conversation we react by means of language and body language to our conversation partner and in so doing signal to him that we are participating in the communication. Above all, the body language that accompanies our conversations has an essential significance here. This body language expresses more about interest, understanding, and acceptance of the conversation partner than verbal language and cannot be underestimated.

With the use of technical media for communication, we must compensate for the lack of body language by means of additional acoustic signals; otherwise, there will be problems with communication. This situation can be observed with every telephone conversation in which acknowledgement normally occurs by means of words and sounds such as »yes,« »mmmhm-mm,« »aha,« »so,« »of course,« and »oh.« If you avoid giving these acknowledgements sometime during a telephone conversation you will find out that you make your conversation partner extremely insecure. Even after a few seconds

your conversation partner will ask a question like »Are you still there?«.

Even the use of a computer can be understood in a certain way as communication—as communication of a person with a machine. This form of communication also requires reactions of the computer in order for the user to understand what the computer is doing, whether it has »understood« an entry, and whether it is still functioning properly.

Just as every action creates a reaction, a multimedia system should also react to the actions of the user. In this way, the user gets the feeling that he is being taken seriously and that he is able to work effectively with the computer.

Studies on the behavior of people who work with computers have identified »tolerance limits« that reflect an attitude of expectation.

1/10 Second
One tenth of a second is the limit for the feeling of the user that the system is reacting to him immediately and is functioning perfectly.

An example of this is the entry of letters or numbers with the keyboard and the immediate corresponding display on the monitor.

1 Second

One second is the limit for the user to maintain the impression that the computer is still reacting properly. A reaction time of the computer that is longer than one second is perceived as an inconvenient delay.

Example: The user clicks a button without some reaction of the system occurring directly.

If a system process lasts longer than two seconds, the computer should signal the user that the process is running properly, for example, by displaying an hourglass, an appropriate text, or a progress indicator that displays the time still required.

For processes that could last longer than one second, offer the user the possibility to abort the procedure.

10 Seconds

As a rule, 10 seconds are the limit to hold the attention of a user. If no clear reaction of the system occurs even after 10 or more seconds, the user gets the impression that something is wrong. In the best case, the user tries again; in a normal case, however, the user will try something different. An example of this is clicking on a navigation element that calls up another screen page. After no more than 10 seconds, most users try again or select an alternative navigation element, or they exit the system.

Internet as Exception

The limits described here are, however, somewhat relative where using the World Wide Web is concerned. Here experienced users (!) accept absolutely even longer reaction times, even if they find the waiting extremely unpleasant. Novices, on the other hand, are rather quick to exit pages that have relatively long load times.

5.2 Types of Reaction

When working with multimedia systems, people expect unconsciously that the system will answer the following questions for them:

- What can I do here?
- What have I already done?
- What will the computer do for me?
- Did the computer understand my action?
- What is the computer doing now?

The user receives an answer to these questions by means of visual and acoustic signals. If these responses don't exist, the user can become insecure and confused.

The best known example of this is a situation in which the computer does not react, and it is not clear to the user whether the machine is still working or has »crashed.« This situation makes the user very insecure and weakens his trust in the reliability of the computer extremely.

Basically, there are **four different ways** in which the system reacts to the user:

1. The system expects an action of the user, for example, clicking on a navigation element. This can be displayed visually through visible highlighting of the clickable element.
2. The system has understood an action of the user and informs him of this by doing something, for example, giving an acoustic signal.
3. The system is busy with an internal process that is not being displayed on the monitor. For example, relatively large picture files are being loaded (from the hard disk or from the Internet) and cannot be displayed immediately. This can be signaled by the cursor changing to an hourglass.
4. The system reports something to the user: an error, a note, or something similar.

When determining how the system should react to actions of the user, you should consider what reaction of the system the target group would normally expect. In addition, the response (feedback) of the computer should be understandable and clear.

1. The feedback of the system should always be consistent. This means that all clickable elements should react in the same manner and the acoustic messages should always be the same.
2. For *each action* of the user, a reaction of the system should follow.
3. Do not mix interactive and static elements with one another in your presentation. Every Web user knows that underscored words are normally hot words. If you also use underscoring to emphasize words, you will confuse the user.
4. Try to fulfill the expectations of the potential user and address him.

5.3 Dialog Elements

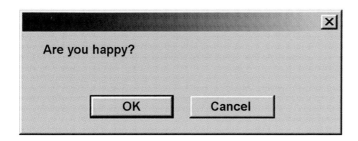

Dialog elements inform the user of something or require him to make a decision to do something or to cause the computer to carry out a process.

When you create direct addressing of the user in linguistic or textual form, you should note the following characteristics:

- Address the user in a manner appropriate to the target group. That is, speak his language.
- Be friendly and polite to the user.
- In dialogs, give the user clear possibilities for decisions. (The user should be able to answer the question »Would you like to exit the program?« with »Yes« or »No,« not with »OK« or »Cancel.«)
- Do not overwhelm the user with too much information or too many selection possibilities. In dialogs, go step-by-step.

Above all, when you create messages and dialogs, think about a real conversation situation.

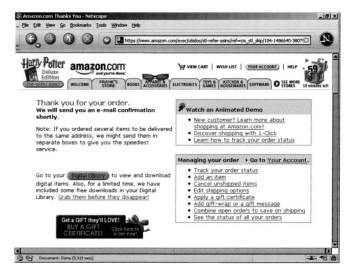

After sending off a form, the user receives a response that signals him that the form has been sent successfully.

When designing dialogs, you should note the following features (according to ISO 9241-10):

Pertinence to Task
The dialog should be appropriate for the task, that is, it should support the user optimally in handling his task and not burden him unnecessarily through preoccupation with the dialog system itself.

Capability for Self-Description
The dialog should be immediately clear and understandable in each of its steps. When the need arises, the user should be able to call up Help that explains the purpose and the possibilities of the dialog. The language and depth of the information should be adapted to the previous knowledge and requirements of the user.

Ability to Control
The dialog should be controllable; that is, the user, not the computer, determines the speed of his procedure. For dialogs, it should be possible to undo entries.

Conformity to Expectations
The dialog should meet the expectations of the user. These expectations result from his work procedures or the experiences that he has already gained in working with the system. All dialogs should be consistent and not force the user to readjust to them constantly.

Tolerance for Errors
The dialog should be able to withstand errors, that is, in the event that the user makes incorrect entries, the computer should not show any uncontrollable reactions; instead, it should make the user aware of the error or correct the error. If there is more than one way to make a correction, the computer should offer these ways to the user as alternatives.

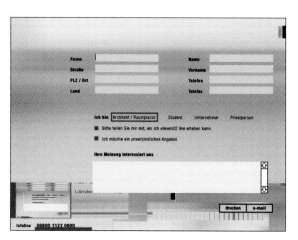

The application form for the USM Company for ordering information material is short, concise, clear, and tailored to the target group. There is nothing that you could leave out. Because of this, the form has such a »simple« effect and motivates the user to fill it out.

5.4 Fitts's Law

»The time to acquire a target is a function of the distance to and the size of the target.«
P. M. Fitts

Fitts's Law, a model of human **psychomotor behavior**, was developed in 1954 and defines how quickly a target on the monitor can be controlled with the cursor of the mouse and which factors influence this.

The nearer an object is to the mouse pointer and the bigger the object is, the simpler it is for the user to control this target. On the other hand, if the object is further away and also relatively small, the effort to control the target becomes increasingly greater because the user must reduce his mouse movement when he approaches the object in order to hit it and not overshoot the target.

A good position for objects is one of the margins of the screen or, better still, one of the corners. They allow themselves to be controlled quickly because the cursor is »captured« by the screen margin. According to Tognazzini (1999), the most easily controllable locations on the screen for a right-handed person are the following:

1. The pixel directly under the actual position of the mouse pointer (reachable under Windows by clicking the right mouse button)
2. The lower right corner
3. The upper left corner
4. The upper right corner
5. The lower left corner

When designing your interaction and navigation elements, note their position and keep in mind that objects are also easier to control if they are not too small.

The navigation elements of Antwerpes are placed on the upper margin and have an appropriate size.

On the site of ABC, the selection of search or keyword with the mouse is somewhat more difficult because of the small size of these elements. Of course, the point is always to find logical compromises. A large element can be selected very easily, but it can »kill« the design of a page. If it is too small, it does indeed step into the background unobtrusively, but it cannot be selected very easily.

5.5 Interaction Checklist

☐ Can the user always recognize and carry out what he can do in each case and what possibilities (options) he has in doing so?

☐ Can the user undo entries?

☐ Is each action of the user followed by a reaction of the system that shows the user that his action has been noticed by the system and that the system is reacting accordingly?

☐ During relatively long waiting periods, does the system show the user that it is doing something or what it is doing?

☐ With respect to file size (= load time), are the files of your Web site optimized?

☐ Are the dialog texts understandable, clear, and polite to the user?

☐ Do the dialogs meet the potential expectations of the target group?

☐ Are the dialogs self-descriptive and understandable?

☐ Are the dialogs short and concise?

☐ Are the dialogs adapted to the tasks or activities of the user?

☐ Does the system tolerate errors?

☐ Can the user adapt the product to his needs?

☐ If problems arise, does the user receive help from the system?

☐ Does the user always have control over the system?

☐ Do your interaction and navigation elements have a good position and size according to Fitts´s law?

6 Emotion

Emotions and motivation are central driving forces behind human actions. For this reason, a good multimedia product addresses users not only on a cognitive level, but also on an emotional one and applies specific motivational strategies.

6.1 Communication and Metamessages

In the 1960s, Joseph Weizenbaum developed a language analysis program that he called ELIZA.

»*The human conversationalist partner would type his portion of the conversation on a typewriter connected to the computer, and the computer, under control of my program, would analyze the message that had been so transmitted to it, compose a response to it in English, and cause the response to be typed on the computer's typewriter.*« (Weizenbaum 1976, 2 f.)

ELIZA reacted to natural language text entries of a user by recognizing keywords in the entries and generating a more or less appropriate »answer« from a database. If ELIZA did not »understand« an entry, that is, if there were no keywords that matched the database, the program turned the entries into questions.

The people involved in testing the program said, after working with the program, that they had the feeling of having had a conversation with the computer. Psychotherapists feared that they might be out of a job. And even after an explanation of how the program functioned, the impression still remained that communication had taken place.

From the experiences with ELIZA (and similar programs that followed), one can conclude that we humans—as social beings—don't require many reactions at all, and especially not high-quality ones,

from a communication partner (in this case the computer) in order to perceive a social situation as a communication situation. A few simple signals and reactions are sufficient to give us the feeling that the computer reacted intentionally to us, that is, it intended something with its reaction.

»*I was startled to see how quickly and how very deeply people conversing with DOCTOR [the ELIZA program playing a psychiatrist] became emotionally involved with the computer and how unequivocally they anthropomorphized it. Once my secretary, who had watched me work on the program for many months and therefore surely knew it to be merely a computer program, started conversing with it. After only a few interchanges with it, she asked me to leave the room. Another time, I suggested I might rig the system so that I could examine all conversations anyone had had with it, say, overnight. I was promptly bombarded with accusations that what I proposed amounted to spying on people's most intimate thoughts; clear evidence that people were conversing with the computer as if it were a person who could be appropriately and usefully addressed in intimate terms. I knew of course that people form all sorts of emotional bonds to machines, for example, to musical instruments, motorcycles, and cars. And I knew from long experi-*

Here is an excerpt from the »communication« of a test person with the ELIZA program of Joseph Weizenbaum. The »answers« of ELIZA are written in capital letters.

»Men are all alike.
IN WHAT WAY
They're always bugging us about something or other.
CAN YOU THINK OF A SPECIFIC EXAMPLE
Well, my boyfriend made me come here.
YOUR BOYFRIEND MADE YOU COME HERE
He says I'm depressed much of the time.
I AM SORRY TO HEAR YOU ARE DEPRESSED
It's true. I am unhappy
DO YOU THINK COMING HERE WILL HELP YOU NOT TO BE UNHAPPY
I need some help, that much seems certain.
WHAT WOULD IT MEAN TO YOU IF YOU GOT SOME HELP
Perhaps I could learn to get along with my mother.
TELL ME MORE ABOUT YOUR FAMILY
My mother takes care of me.
WHO ELSE IN YOUR FAMILY TAKES CARE OF YOU
My father.
YOUR FATHER
You are like my father in some ways.
WHAT RESEMBLANCE DO YOU SEE
You are not very aggressive but I think you don't want me to notice that.
WHAT MAKES YOU THINK I AM NOT VERY AGGRESSIVE
You don't argue with me.
WHY DO YOU THINK I DON'T ARGUE WITH YOU
You are afraid of me.
DOES IT PLEASE YOU TO BELIEVE I AM AFRAID OF YOU
My father is afraid of everybody.
WHAT ELSE COMES TO YOUR MIND WHEN YOU THINK OF YOUR FATHER
Bullies.
DOES THAT HAVE ANYTHING TO DO WITH THE FACT THAT YOUR BOYFRIEND MADE YOU COME HERE«

Joseph Weizenbaum (1966): Eliza. A Computer Program For the Study of Natural Language Communication Between Man and Machine. In: Communications of the ACM Volume 9, Number 1 (January 1966), 36–35

ence that the strong emotional ties many programmers have to their computers are often formed after only short exposures to their machines. What I had not realized is that extremely short exposures to a relatively simple computer program could induce powerful delusional thinking in quite normal people. This insight led me to attach new importance to questions of the relationship between the individual and the computer, and hence to resolve to think about them.« (Weizenbaum 1976, 6 f.)

The communications researchers Byron Reeves and Clifford Nass made similar observations. They were able to prove impressively that we transfer our social and communicative behavior to interactive media. In addition, we project our expectations to the computer.

And although we know that we are dealing only with a machine, we react to the computer similarly as we would to human beings: we are happy if people are friendly to us; we are insulted if people ignore us; we are mistrustful if we think someone is lying to us; and we expect an appropriate reaction to our behavior from the person to whom we are talking. We expect exactly these (and other) forms of behavior from the computer.

An extreme example makes this point clear. A few years ago there was a video circulating on the Web in which you could see an office worker pounding his computer keyboard furiously with his fist and then finally he throws the keyboard and the monitor off the desk. This video—**Bad Day**—was produced and distributed in 1996 by the US company Loronix, a manufacturer of software for surveillance cameras. It dealt with a play-acted scene, not a real situation. Nonetheless, it gives many viewers an excellent opportunity for emotional identification. Only a very few computer users have let their frustrations run wild in this form, but the situation of reacting strongly to errors of the machine or to an inadequate operator interface is a familiar experience for many.

Using computers evokes deep-seated social behavior patterns. In a social communication situation as is portrayed in Bad Day, the expectations of the user are obviously badly neglected. The computer does not react (the silent partner on the telephone makes us nervous), it »crashes« (the person to whom we are talking leaves in the middle of a conversation, without giving an explanation or saying good-bye), or the computer does not »understand« the entries of the user (the person to whom we are talking asks the same old question again and again).

»*Every communication has a content aspect and a relationship aspect, such that the latter determines the former and therefore is a metacommunication.*« Paul Watzlawick

Metacommunication

These social behavior patterns are related to a phenomenon that communication researchers call metacommunication. When we communicate with one another, we are not just exchanging pure information; rather, we are always giving signals as to what we think of our communication partner, whether we mean what we are saying seriously or ironically, and how we assess the other person and ourselves in the social situation. By speaking, we always do more than »transmit« only a spoken message—we behave through our speaking actions.

The communication researcher Paul Watzlawick has designated this metacommunication as a relationship level that always influences the understanding of the content level. *How* we say something, and in what context we say something, plays a significant role.

If someone is called »old man« by a friend, he will feel differently about it if his boss calls him that. Humor, irony, and insults can only be understood appropriately through the context in which they occur, and the rest of the communication is also strongly influenced by metamessages.

Metacommunication often also occurs without words or »between the spoken words.« For example, if you look at your watch during a conversation, the person to whom you are talking could interpret this behavior as a sign that you are bored. Whether you mean this or not is irrelevant in this situation. The »listener« determines what he hears, that is, how he interprets your behavior.

The German psychologist Schulz von Thun described this state of affairs with his model of the four pages of a message. Accordingly, every communication has four levels: the objective content (the topic about which I am providing information), the self-revelation (what I am telling about myself), the relationship level (what I think about you and what our relationship is), and the appeal (what I would like to make you do). The objective level plays only a partial role in communication situations. And obviously this is also the case with man-machine interaction.

Illustration: Friedemann Schulz von Thun

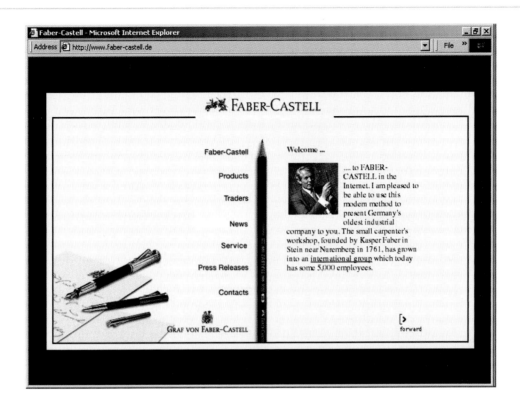

Faber-Castell - Microsoft Internet Explorer

Address http://www.faber-castell.de File

FABER-CASTELL

Faber-Castell

Products

Traders

News

Service

Press Releases

Contacts

GRAF VON FABER-CASTELL

Welcome ...

.... to FABER-
CASTELL in the
Internet. I am pleased to
be able to use this
modern method to
present Germany's
oldest industrial
company to you. The small carpenter's
workshop, founded by Kasper Faber in
Stein near Nuremberg in 1761, has grown
into an international group which today
has some 5,000 employees.

[>
forward

Example FABER-CASTELL

Even the material on Web pages is perceived by people not only on the objective level, but also on the relationship level. The metamessages are interpreted by the users—often unconsciously. So Web sites can signal seriousness, dynamic force, unprofessionalism, frivolity, ignorance, and other things. A good example of this is the Web site of the FABER-CASTELL Company. Besides the actual content (products, novelties, company presentations), the way in which information is presented signals elegance and tastefulness, seriousness and tradition. It is the type of presentation, the beige colored background, the use of dark green, the font, the coat of arms, the picture of the very serious looking gentleman, and the clear structure of the page. These signals are not necessarily perceived consciously; instead, they often are perceived unconsciously and, for this reason, are more effective. They work as metamessages that users relate not only to the Web site itself, but also automatically to the company and the products.

When designing your products, take the time to get a clear idea of the implicit metamessages that you want to express and create them very consciously through the type of presentation.

233

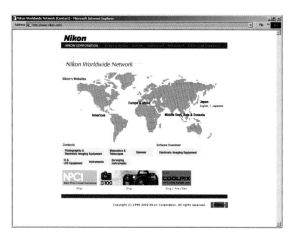

Two start pages signal their visitors immediately what awaits them. While the clothing company HUGO BOSS expresses an elegant and posh image by means of reserved and tasteful Web material, the start page of the PEPSI COMPANY embodies colorfulness, the joy of living, and dynamic force. What are the metamessages here? And what would you expect as a visitor to the pages that follow?

The start page of NIKON contains multiple metamessages that revel themselves only with a closer look: internationality, an unobtrusive restraint, a great variety of offerings, and service capability. BURGER KING is a complete contrast to this page, with a very direct approach, but one that contains more metamessages than just objective information about what it has to offer.

234

The First Impression Is Decisive

In the analysis of a person or a thing, the first and last impressions are especially dominant and remain fixed in memory. They displace all other impressions in their meaning and memorableness. This effect is called the **primacy effect** or recency effect. For example, after an audience listens to a lecture, they remember the beginning and the end better than the intermediate part. That's why the »clincher« is important. These effects also apply to your multimedia product, whether it's a CD-ROM or a Web site. The beginning must sink in. It must motivate the user and leave a positive impression. Here the first impression essentially determines the assessment of the whole. At a glance, your users get an impression of you and your material and they decide instantaneously whether it is worthwhile to deal with what you have to offer.

The start page of the FORT WORTH OPERA reflects a typical opera atmosphere by means of pictures and the design of the page. The start page of AXA Insurance doesn't exactly invite you to get to know their products better. And the YAHOO! page communicates a wealth of offerings, but perhaps also the impression of being »worn out« by the overabundance.

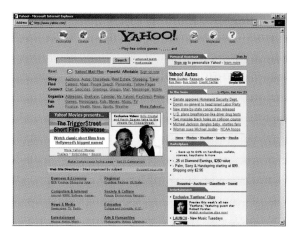

6.2 Motivation, Goals, Practicality

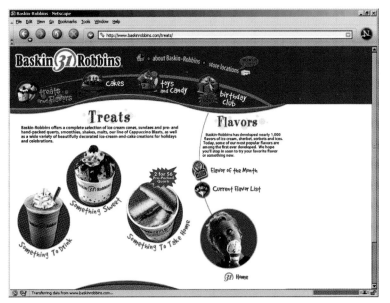

of bed in the morning even though it is cold, wet, and unpleasant outside and, in bed, it is comfortably warm. The answer is that various goals drive people to do something, even if it is unpleasant. A motive is, therefore, a reason to want to achieve a certain goal, and motivation is an inner frame of mind and a dynamic toward this.

Frequently, an intrinsic motivation (one triggered from within) urges us on, but also motivations that are controlled from outside influence us and our actions. In advertising, for example, the motivation generated from the outside (extrinsic) plays an essential role.

Because people are beings full of emotions and desires, not information processing machines, working with multimedia information systems, Web sites, and tutorials also depends greatly on the emotional acceptance of the particular product.

Only a positive emotional attitude makes the use of the multimedia product effective. As *Frederik Vester* presented in his fundamental work *Denken, Lernen, Vergessen* (*Thinking, Learning, Forgetting*), it is only this positive attitude that makes it possible to learn effectively or to grasp information. Positive emotions, fun, interest, curiosity, and excitement create a physical hormone condition that enables our brain to process effectively those things that we have perceived.

Everything that we do, we do with a specific intention. Motivation is the mainspring of human behavior. Goals and motives cause us to act and make our behavior understandable. Even a »purposeless« game provides relaxation or cultivates social contact.

The American psychologist *William James* founded motivation research in 1890 with the question of how a person manages to get out

Learning without fun and personal interest is torture and just as laborious as the use of a multimedia information system that presents pure facts dryly and inflexibly. The Web site that wants to be noticed hardly has a chance to be used if it does not motivate its visitors to continue working with it.

Basically, a product has a motivating effect if it is designed to be oriented to the target group, if it can be operated intuitively and is structured clearly, if it offers useful information, and if it speaks to the user in his language. In addition, motivating elements make the product easier to use and make its use more effective.

It is also true that where the carefully directed use of motivating elements is concerned, the first question is the one concerning the target group and its expectations. Should motivation occur by means of a prospect of enjoyment (for example, food), of prestige (for example, hobbies and status symbols), or by means of promising security and protection (for example, life insurance)?

6.3 Curiosity

People are curious by nature. You can use this characteristic to motivate. The discovery of a multimedia product has a strong motivation factor for many users who initially tackle a topic by »rummaging around.« This experience is interesting in the long run, however, only if the user actually discovers something interesting, that is, something new that is also significant to the user.

The two start pages pictured here use a black background and attempt to arouse the visitor's curiosity through image and text.

The page of ALL ABOUT EVE is mysterious because of the picture and also the navigation elements (past, now, future).

With the MUNICIPAL UTILITIES OF KARLSRUHE, the visitor is asked if the tap water of his city is drinkable. Because this question is relevant to a resident of Karlsruhe, it invites the visitor to »enter« the site.

The material from WOLFORD also arouses curiosity through its unusual design.

With these examples, however, the limitations of these strategies also become clear: things can go wrong if the user becomes confused instead of becoming curious.

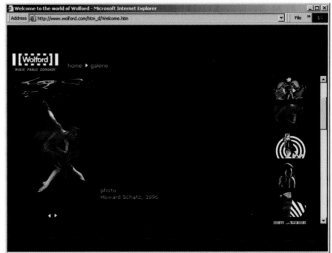

The home page of the German JESUS FREAKS warns expressly against entering the Web site. It is exactly this warning that arouses the curiosity of the youthful target group.

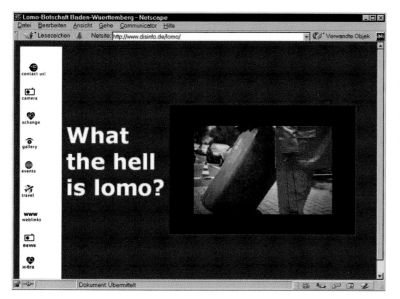

The start page of the Lomographischen Gesellschaft Baden-Württemberg (LOMOGRAPHIC SOCIETY OF BADEN-WÜRTTEMBERG) greets the visitor by asking just what exactly Lomo is. A click that leads to the pages that follow promises an answer.

6.4 Attracting Attention

Attention
Interest
Desire
Action

A proven advertising strategy from advertising psychology is the so-called AIDA formula. This model describes how to convey an advertising message appropriately. The AIDA formula consists of four steps, whereby each individual step builds on the one before it.

- In the first step, an attempt is made to attract attention (A = **attention**) of a target group with lightning speed, for example, by means of a visual key stimulus.
- After that, the interest (I = **interest**) for the matter should be aroused and amplified by providing information that is relevant and interesting to the target group.
- The next step consists of awakening desires (D = **desire**) to have something or to do something.
- And finally, in the fourth step, an action (A = **action**) should result, preferably a purchase.

Use this strategy to get the attention of the user for your multimedia product.

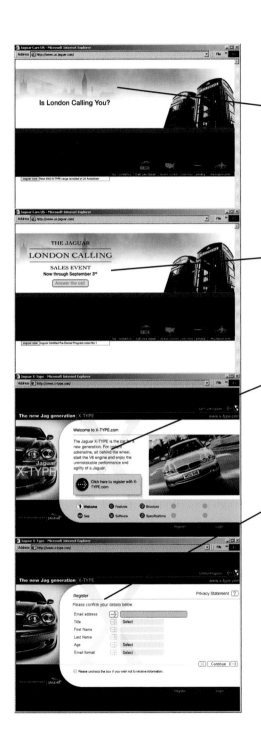

Attracting Attention

The skyline of London, two red telephone booths, and the question »Is London Calling You?« are intended to arouse curiosity. Images and text are very eye catching and are comprehended quickly.

Arousing Interest

Once attention has been attracted, the user is directed to a sales event and asked to accept the telephone call from London.

Developing a Desire

The next page then promises to lead to a very special car—exclusive and exciting. One click on the green button offers access to a select circle of prospective buyers.

Triggering Action

Finally, the user is able to join the »select« prospective buyers and to get special information on the product. In order to do this, the user must enter personal information on a form.

6.5 Practicality and Clarity

*»The benefit of information lies in the selection, not in its abundance;
it lies in the relevance, not in the speed of transmission.«* Frederic Vester

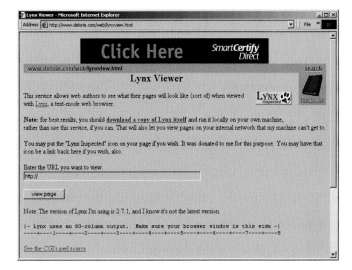

You are surfing in the World Wide Web and you come to a page that asks you to click on a button. Do you click? In a fraction of a second you reflect on whether it is worthwhile to click on the button. How long will it take for the new page to be loaded? What will it contain? Where will this click take me? Is it worthwhile? Or will I end up at a dead end (*under construction*)?

Tell the user why he should click, and he will be more willing to do it. Offer him something that is worth his while. And also tell him what it will cost.

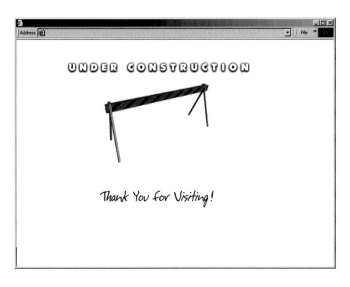

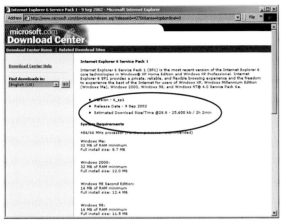

The Download Center of MICROSOFT provides exact information about the files that you can download and about the time that is required for downloading these files. In addition, a short text informs you about the function of the file.

On his Web site, *Jacob Nielsen* describes clearly and in detail how you can order the Alertbox E-Mail Newsletter and what happens when you order it. In addition, he says how you can cancel the newsletter.

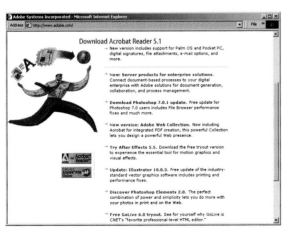

The ADOBE COMPANY provides brief descriptions of various things that you can download. In this way, you know what is hidden behind the link. Additional information on file size and transmission time appears on the pages that follow.

6.6 Humor

The use of humor and wit can facilitate motivation considerably and, in so doing, make a product easier to use. In this example, the Mozart opera *Cosi fan tutte* is told in a very original manner and offers even the Mozart connoisseur new and interesting insights into the life of the Austrian composer.

But be careful: not every Mozart admirer likes this way of dealing with the esteemed composer. Humor can also create misunderstanding and strong disapproval!

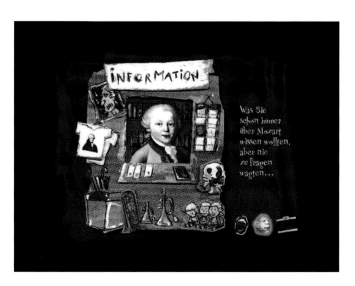

Translation picture above:
What you always wanted to know about Mozart, but were afraid to ask …

Translation picture below:
Mozart to eat. Believe it or not—this label is made of chocolate!

Translation picture above:
- Don Alfonso
- Age: 62 years
- Hanging around in coffee houses
- Weaving webs of intrigue
- Philosophizing

Humor is a very individual quality and, when used in the wrong way, can achieve exactly the opposite of its intention. Not everyone who owns a poodle will find the Web site of JOE BOXER to be funny. Applying humor in the wrong way can hurt you because it angers the user.

Keep in mind, too, that humor is influenced strongly by culture. An impressive example of this is the English group MONTY PYTHON.

- Pay attention to the tastes of your target group. Note cultural differences.
- Never make fun of others.
- Don't make jokes about your audience.
- Be extremely cautious with religious, political, or sexual topics.
- The humor should be related to your topic.
- Your humor should be distinguished by lightness and (self-) irony.
- Your humor should not trigger any negative feelings.
- Your humor should not digress from the actual topic and should not become an end in itself, unless that is the goal of your product.

6.7 Emotion Checklist

☐ What do you want to communicate with what you have to offer?

☐ What metamessages are your users supposed to perceive?

☐ What visual signals (such as visual symbols, images, use of color, language, text design) do you use to communicate the metamessage?

☐ What emotions do you want to trigger in the user?

☐ What first impression do your users probably have when they first see what you have to offer?

☐ What first impression are your visitors supposed to have?

☐ Do you make clear to the user the advantage that he will have by using your product?

☐ Do you tell the user what the result or consequences of his actions will be?

☐ Do you motivate the user with things that he likes and that are familiar to him?

☐ Is the design of your product adapted to the expectations and preferences of your target group?

☐ Does the »first impression« of your product help your potential user to have a positive attitude toward your product?

☐ Are there possibilities for stimulating the natural curiosity of the users?

☐ Do you think it makes sense to proceed according to the »AIDA formula?« And how concretely?

☐ Does the use of humorous elements appear appropriate to you?

☐ What type of humor is the target group likely to accept?

☐ Does the humor offend any religious or other personal feelings?

☐ Is the humor also acceptable in other cultures?

☐ Is the humor appropriate for the product?

7 Intercultural Screen Design

This chapter presents the meaning that a culture has for its members. Because culture always also has to do with identity and is very important to people, you should consider cultural characteristics when designing screens. Various features of cultures are presented and illustrated with examples of how pages should be designed for specific cultures.

7.1 Culture and Identity

»A culture is understood to be an identifiable group with shared beliefs and common experiences, with a sense of values that are connected to these experiences, and with an interest in a common historic background.«
R.W. Brislin

Every person belongs to a culture. Because of this, he possesses specific values and preferences that are deeply anchored in his culture and a special way of perceiving the world and interpreting experiences. Even if people are very different, still there are specific characteristics in each culture that apply to almost all members of this culture.

Thus Italians tend to like to talk a lot and to use their entire body while doing so. Americans are normally very pragmatic. Finns are considered to be quiet and reserved. Germans tend to be objective and orderly. And Russians tend toward melancholy. Japanese are considered to be polite and community oriented.

Behind these general statements is the realization that people are not only influenced, but are also greatly characterized, by their culture—that is, by their language, their social contacts, their rules of behavior; but also by celebrations, rituals, the climate, and the things that they eat. »Generalising on national traits breaks down with individuals but stands firm with large numbers« (Lewis 1999, 33), writes Richard Lewis in his book *When Cultures Collide*.

Geert Hofstede calls culture a »collective programming of the intellect that distinguishes the members of one group or category of people from others« (Hofstede 2001, 4). Such everyday things as the way people eat, their greetings, or their personal hygiene belong to these distinguishing characteristics.

The way in which we communicate with other people (relationship oriented or object oriented), our perception of space (for example, the amount of space between people who are conversing) and time (punctual or extremely flexible), taste (bright colors or unobtrusive dark hues), the relationship to nature, appreciation for culturally specific artifacts (stories, fairy tales, songs), the significance of family, and many other things influence us greatly—mostly unconsciously. And these unconscious cultural values and ways of behaving determine our perception, that is, our attention, our thinking and speaking, our preferences, our feelings, and our memories.

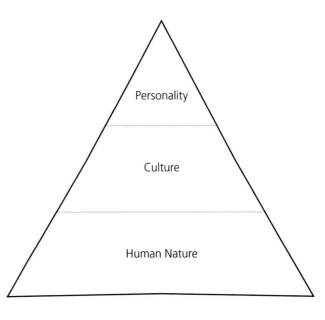

The pyramid of Hofstede represents the three levels of a person. The basis is formed by biological nature, which is inherited and is the same for all people. To this nature belong basic emotions—fear, surprise, revulsion, sorrow, anger, and joy—and the desire for life in a society. The second level is formed by the culture. It is learned and its rules and values are binding within a specific group. The third level is the personality of the specific individual that is based on experiences and things that are learned individually.

Generally, we do not notice our own culture because we experience it matter-of-factly, because everyone acts more or less the same way. Only when we are confronted by a different culture, for example, by living abroad, do we discover—often painfully—that our values and ways of behaving are not perfectly natural for other people. We discover that these people perceive many things differently. We discover that, in part, other things are important and significant to them and therefore they behave entirely differently in specific situations. And it is often difficult for us to recognize these different people as equals because they appear to be so foreign and incomprehensible.

What does all that have to do with screen design? When we look at Web pages, we see more than the actual information. We also perceive the manner in which the contents are presented to us, how we are addressed, and what topics are placed in the foreground. Even colors, images, and the general design of the Web material send a message.

For example, addressing the user of a Web site in the USA or Italy in a very direct, head-on manner can be regarded as completely appropriate, while this form of address is more likely to scare off people in an Asian culture because it is considered to be too direct and inappropriate. And the green pages of a British environmental organization might be rejected in Arab countries because green is the color of the Islamic religion and for this reason may only be used selectively. The French national colors on a Web site are assuredly well received in France, but can evoke very mixed feelings in one of the former colonies. A South American, for whom the explanation of the relationship level is a top priority in social interaction, won't be able to do much with an intensive presentation of pure objective information from a company, because he wants to know first of all whether he can even trust this company.

While some Web pages come to the point quickly with a clear structure, others present their contents in a more reserved and frivolous manner. While some pages are very factual and objective, others send out stronger emotional signals.

A good screen design should always take the characteristics of the culture of the particular target group into consideration. Addressing people selectively also means addressing them within the cultural identity in which they are deeply

»Perception, and indeed every perception, is active designing. This designing is not only in the sense that a person classifies mentally the infinite abundance of the physical stimuli that register with him and that are picked up physiologically by receptors. Such classifications include: important and unimportant, significant and insignificant, figure and ground. Also, included in human perception constantly and fundamentally is the entire wealth of subjective experience, embedded in the entire personality structure of a person, including that which his development as well as his material and cultural environment has given him with regard to the way he views things and the way he thinks. If man experiences the world through perception, then he does so neither objectively-neutral nor passively. Rather, with each perception the entire person is involved actively, projectively, and designedly. Thus perception is not only determined biologically, but to a great extent shaped socially and culturally. This means: people of different cultures perceive the world in their own way.« Gerhard Maletzke

rooted. Something that functions well in your own culture can fail in a different culture. That which is strange or foreign is initially unpleasant for most people, while that which is familiar is regarded as inspiring trust.

No matter what you want to achieve with your material, you should first answer the following questions:

- What things have a special value in this particular culture?
- What is important to the people; what is less important?
- What do they like and what do they dislike?
- How do the people communicate with each other? How do they behave?
- How do they see themselves and how do they want to be seen by others?

- What do they tell other people when they are asked about their culture?
- How do they deal with symbols and what are the typical symbols of this culture?
- How do these people deal with images and colors?

Answering these questions could sharpen your image of your target group. If you apply these findings selectively by addressing the target group appropriately, you will reach these people in their deepest identity.

7.2 Cultural Manifestations

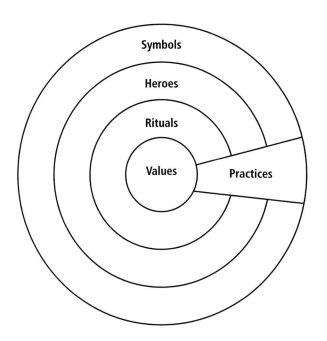

Illustration according to Hofstede 2001, 9

In his *onion model*, Geert Hofstede describes the different ways in which cultures manifest themselves.

For him, **values** form the core of a culture, that is, feelings that are assessed as negative or positive, such as good—bad, clean—dirty, beautiful—ugly, or normal—abnormal. Values are conveyed implicitly in earliest childhood and later are very permanently anchored. Value judgments are frequently made intuitively and instinctively. We do not *decide* that something is bad or ugly, rather we *sense* it as bad or ugly, and this feeling is so deeply rooted that only with great difficul-

ty can we discuss it logically or even change these values. Value judgments appear to us to be so obvious that we always regard those value judgments of people of other cultures that contradict our value judgments as something negative.

One area in which the values of a culture are expressed is in **rituals**. Rituals are »collective activities that are actually superfluous for achieving the desired goals, but within a culture they count as socially necessary: for this reason they are performed for their own sake.« (Hofstede 2001, 8 f.) Rituals are forms of social cohabitation, such as greetings. But they also identify the individual with the society and strengthen the identity of a society. A lot of rituals have social or religious bases, such as seasonal celebrations—Christmas, Easter, or the Muslim Ramadan; family celebrations—baptism, confirmation, weddings, or funerals; or national celebrations—such as the French national holiday (July 14th) or the American independence day (July 4th).

All cultures have **heroes** who possess a role model character and who serve as a point of orientation. There are historic heroes—such as Mohandas Karamchand Gandhi (India), Jeanne d'Arc (France) or Wilhelm Tell (Switzerland); the (much more short-lived) current heroes—such as those from the world of sports (Michael Schumacher in

Germany) or from the music business (Michael Jackson, USA); and the fictitious heroes—such as Asterix and Obelix (France) or the Peanuts (USA).

Finally, every culture has its specific symbols, such as traditional costumes, flags, hairstyles, or special status symbols. Symbols are essentially more »fleeting« than the other cultural manifestations and for this reason form the outermost layer of the onion.

Rituals, heroes, and symbols are visible in **practice**, but their cultural significance lies deeper and is not clear to the outside observer, because this significance »lies exactly and exclusively in the way in which these practices are interpreted by insiders« (Hofstede 2001, 9).

For intercultural Web design, it is absolutely necessary to become aware of the manifestations of a culture. These manifestations have a strong identification function for the members of the culture and define their affiliation with the specific culture.

The Web site of the White House of the USA shows *the* symbol of the US Americans—the Stars and Stripes—and uses this symbol to signal both patriotism and the democratic fundamental convictions of the American Declaration of Independence.

On its Thai Web site, the KODAK Company shows typical national costumes and in so doing addresses the visitor on an emotional level.

256

At KODAK Belgium, we find the famous landmark of Brussels, »Männeken Piss,« who represents a kind of hero in Belgium.

The site of Wools of New Zealand reflects very specific symbols of the country: elements of the untouched New Zealand nature—mountains, sheep, and green landscapes.

KODAK Greece shows a typical Greek harbor, which for Greeks is more than just a harbor. It is also a meeting place; symbol of earning a living; and gateway to the Mediterranean Sea, which has often played an important role in Greek history.

KODAK Netherlands shows the canals, narrow houses, and ubiquitous bicycles, as well as the windmills and tulip fields. For the viewers in the Netherlands, this is part of the homeland and is therefore cast as very familiar and positive.

The pages of the Japanese company YAKULT differ in their material in the Japanese and English (international) versions. The Japanese pages take into consideration the specific preferences of the Japanese, such as the striking use of pastel colors (here: pink and yellow), the integration of comic figures, and the use of Japanese characters as an aesthetic element. In contrast, the international pages are deliberately designed austerely by using a white background, shorter text passages, and images that are more reserved in their color scheme.

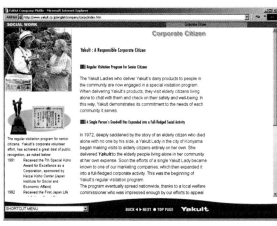

259

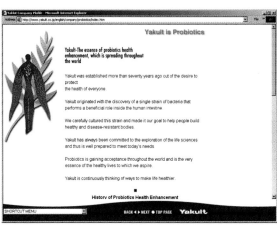

7.3 Lewis´s Three Basic Cultures

»The several hundred national and regional cultures of the world can be roughly classified into three groups: task-oriented, highly organised planners (linear-active); people-oriented, loquacious interrelators (multi-active); introvert, respect-oriented listeners (reactive). Italians see Germans as stiff and time-dominated; Germans see Italians gesticulating in chaos; the Japanese observes and quietly learns from both.« Richard Lewis

The British linguist and director of an institute for intercultural communication, Richard Lewis, divides the cultures of the world roughly into three categories (Lewis 2000): linear-active, multi-active, and reactive cultures.

People in **linear-active cultures** like to make plans and also make a great effort to stick to these plans. For them, order is important, they are reliable, correct, and punctual. In discussions and negotiations, they are objective, they rely on data and facts, and they argue logically. They are good listeners. People of this culture are task oriented and methodical; they frequently keep their professional lives and private lives separate. They tend to be introverted, quiet, and objective. According to Lewis, Germans and Swiss are above all liner-active, followed by the white Protestant Americans of Anglo-Saxon ancestry. After them come Scandinavians, Austrians, Britons, Canadians, and New Zealanders.

In contrast to the linear-active cultures are the **multi-active cultures**. People of these cultures are often versatilely active, do several things at a time, and are always »on duty.« They rarely keep their professional lives and private lives separate, they are extremely flexible and therefore don't often stick to plans and agreements. Multi-active people tend not to be punctual. They are not objective; rather, they are people-oriented, emotional, curious, and sociable. They are excellent speakers, but they are not very good listeners. They frequently argue emotionally, not objectively; they are never at a loss for an excuse; they interrupt frequently in a conversation; and they have an elaborate body language. According to Lewis, the Latin American cultures are the most multi-active, followed by the Arab cultures, the Africans, and the people of India. In

linear-active	multi-active	reactive
• introvert	• extrovert	• introvert
• patient	• impatient	• patient
• quiet	• talkative	• silent
• minds own business	• inquisitive	• respectful
• likes privacy	• gregarious	• good listener
• plans ahead methodically	• plans grand outline only	• looks at general principles
• does one thing at a time	• does several things at once	• reacts
• works fixed hours	• works any hours	• flexible hours
• punctual	• unpunctual	• punctual
• dominated by timetables and schedules	• timetable unpredictable	• reacts to partner's timetable
• compartmentalises projects	• lets one project influence another	• sees whole picture
• sticks to plans	• changes plans	• makes slight changes
• sticks to facts	• juggles facts	• statements are promises
• gets information from statistics, reference books, database	• gets first-hand (oral) information	• uses both
• job-oriented	• people-oriented	
• unemotional	• emotional	• people-oriented
• works within department	• gets round all departments	• quietly caring
• follows correct procedures	• pulls strings	• all departments
• accepts favours reluctantly	• seeks favours	• inscrutable, calm
• delegates to competent colleques	• delegates to relations	• protects face of other
• completes action chains	• completes human transactions	• delegates to reliable people
• likes fixed agendas	• interrelates everything	• reacts to partner
• brief on telephone	• talks for hours	• thoughtful
• uses memoranda	• rarely writes memos	• summarises well
• respects officialdom	• seeks out (top) key person	• plans slowly
• dislikes losing face	• has ready excuses	• ultra honest
• confronts with logic	• confronts emotionally	• must not lose face
• limited body language	• unrestricted body language	• avoids confrontation
• rarely interrupts	• interrupts frequently	• subtle body language
• separates social/ professional	• interweaves social/ professional	• doesn't interrupt
		• connects social and professional

Source: Richard D. Lewis: When Cultures Collide. London: Nicholas Brealay Publ.1996, 41

The site of the Finnish government reflects the reactive culture strongly. The pages are very unobtrusive and reserved in the selection of color and in design.

Europe they are primarily the Mediterranean peoples (Spanish, Italians, and Greeks).

The third category is that of the **reactive cultures**. People of these cultures are, like the multi-active people, also people oriented and have a considerate interest in their fellow men. They are flexible, but take into consideration the schedule of their partner, and they behave with extreme respect. People of reactive cultures are attentive listeners; they tend to be introverted and quiet to uncommunicative. Their body language is very subtle, and for people of other cultures, they often give the impression of being »impenetrable« and unfathomable because the unobtrusive signals in their communication are often overlooked. Countries of greatly reactive cultures are Japan, China, Taiwan, and, in the Euro-

pean area Finland and Turkey. Also Swedes and people from Great Britain sometimes act reactively.

What happens then if people of a multi-active culture communicate with linear-active or reactive people? Both sides will feel uncomfortable after a while because the data orientation of the linear-active people scares off the multi-active people and appears inhuman to them, and the linear-active people will be irritated by the emotionality and »illogic« of the multi-active people. For the multi-active people, relationships are more important than prescribed goals; the linear-active people want to achieve the specified goals. And the members of a reactive culture feel »run over« by the speed and emotionality of the multi-active culture, while they perceive the people of the linear-active culture as unsocial.

The irritations that can be observed in communication situations between US Americans and Japanese, between Germans and Italians, between the British and French also occur on the Web when pages reflect cultural characteristics—and they do this automatically because they have been created by people of a specific culture. The sensational invitation on the home page of a US business to take a look at the advantages of a product can give the impression in a reactive culture—for example, in Finland— of being »blurted out.« For example, in China or the Philippines it is customary to receive information about the communication partner (for example, the company) initially before getting into the contents and products. Trust must be established first. The emotion triggering, playful pages of an Italian company

The multi-active culture of Jamaica is expressed in the tourist pages of that country. Here extroversion, sociability, and exuberance prevail.

can be perceived as garrulous and chaotic in the German speaking part of Switzerland. The strict, orderly, and hierarchical structuring of a German Web site does not necessarily come across as positive in all cultures; instead, it sometimes has a sterile and impersonal effect.

It is especially important to take note of cultural taboos. Especially in the area of religion, people of all cultures normally react extremely sensitively to violations of taboos.

So it is important to take into consideration cultural characteristics, especially as far as communication behavior is concerned. The examples on the following pages can give you some ideas. For details, see the list of references to related literature at the end of this chapter.

The linear-active culture of the Germans is expressed on the pages of the Lower House of the German Parliament: clear structures and facts predominate here.

7.4 NESTLÉ's Pages Customized for Specific Countries

The Swiss food conglomerate NESTLÉ appears world wide under the motto »Good Food, Good Life.« Their Web sites are structured and designed very differently in the various countries and in most cases they show a great interest in each particular culture. The way the company presents itself and its products is also as specifically varied as the topics of the Web material. The nationally oriented pages reflect each particular culture, give familiar signals (such as certain colors or symbols), take into consideration the values specific to the culture (such as the role of the family or the individual), and show intensive interest in current trends.

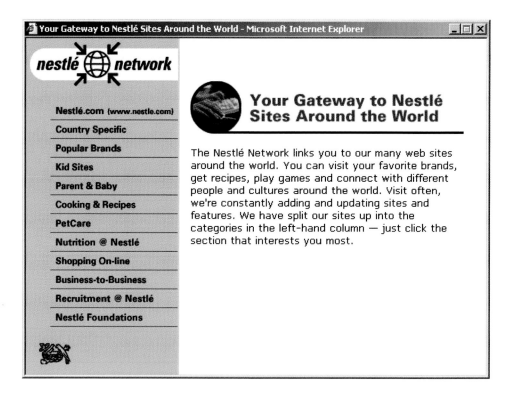

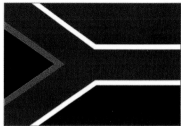

The multicultural society of **South Africa** is reflected in the pictures of the Web site. The message reads: we're doing something for the development of the country; we're contributing to peaceful coexistence. The pages communicate friendliness, harmony, and partnership, not only of the company with the people in South Africa, but of the South Africans among themselves.

The color design of the **Australian** site reflects the national flag. A photo on the home page shows a family that is running across the seashore, enjoying life to the fullest. In this way, the photo refers to a typical Australian weekend pastime: going on an outing with the family to the great outdoors.

It is not a product or a mood that plays a significant role here; rather, service and support in every form. »Use our Australian Institute of Sport Program,« »Give Your Family a Break,« or »Win over $ 20,000« is what it says there. Everywhere there is something to win, to try out; everywhere the visitor receives interesting offers. By means of the

icon with the silverware, the visitor comes to the area *Good Food, Good Life* and finds recipes there. In the area *Coffee,* there are short films for downloading. Australia as friendly service society (»What can I do for you?«) reappears in this way too on the NESTLÉ site.

Sports play a big role in Australia and rate highly enough on the site to have their own area. On the topic of fitness and *mind power* there are extensive offerings. The enjoyment of coffee has its own special area. The Nescafé Cafés also exist virtually on the Web, naturally with many useful things to offer. There are separate areas for children and

young people, and pets are also given a lot of consideration.

Astonishingly, the original inhabitants of Australia—the Aborigines—are not taken into consideration here, although they have become an important topic of public discussion in the last few years.

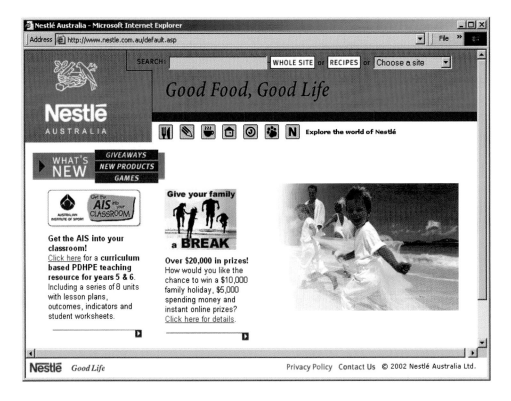

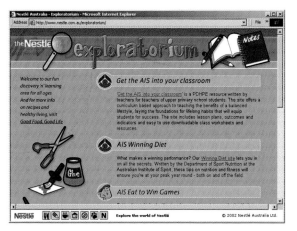

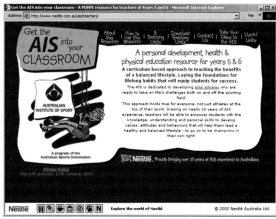

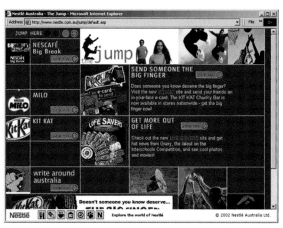

The **German** Web pages of NESTLÉ are clearly structured, somewhat sober and cool, with straight lines, and orderly—all characteristics that are attributed to the Germans again and again. The general color scheme is extremely unobtrusive, but colorful photos are used.

The material has a relatively formal effect; visitors are addressed with the formal form for »you« (»Sie«) and the text has a rather abstract, slightly impersonal character. As a whole, the material is strongly topic and object oriented.

National pride has a somewhat negative connotation in Germany;

because of their history, most Germans have an ambivalent relationship with national symbols such as flag or anthem. Maybe that's why the colors of the German flag (black, red, gold) do not appear, in contrast to the NESTLÉ pages of other countries.

The site takes up topics that play a big role in Germany: good nutrition, fitness, but also enjoyment of life (naturally only a healthy one) that is expressed on the home page through the photo of the couple at breakfast—a situation which most Germans associate with a very pleasant time.

The products of the company are in the background and appear every now and then rather unobtrusively. The target group is primarily young people and families; however, there is also information for older people, children, and people who suffer from allergies.

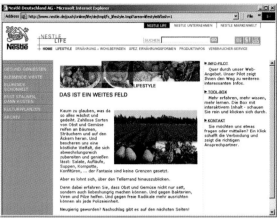

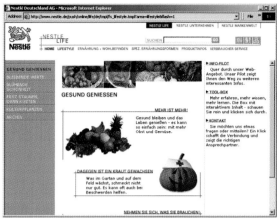

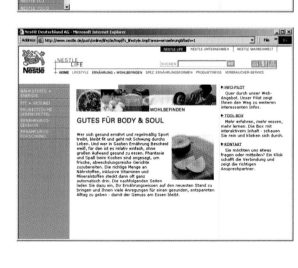

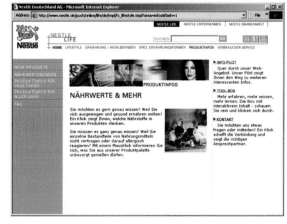

270

The **Russian** pages of NESTLÉ show a very reserved design; they are extremely »heavy on text« and contain only a few pictures. The reason for this is surely first of all that the infrastructure of Internet access in Russia is still underdeveloped and images require a relatively long loading time. In spite of this, the Web material attempts to send signals that try to address people on an emotional level.

One example would be the use of the Russian national colors white, blue, and red, on the start page. A picture of two children is a reminder of the short Russian summer. Two Russian women with whom I viewed these pages were reminded spontaneously of their childhood. The characteristic, very special culture is very important to most Russians and the word tradition rates highly. NESTLÉ picks this up and shows examples of the company's support of cultural events, such as the Chekhov Festival performances. It is pointed out that the cultivation of Russian tradition is a very important goal of the company. This interest in tradition goes to the extent that products have the names of well-known fairy tale characters.

The Web sites of NESTLÉ **Caribbean** address especially young people and children. Bright, friendly colors and photos of people enjoying life are intended to express the Caribbean experience. For the children there is a special play area—*Neskids Corner*—and even pets are looked after especially in *Friskies Pet Club*.

The **Philippines** is the most un-Asian country in Asia. The culture was formed by the Spanish colonization of over 350 years and by the strong influence of the USA after the Second World War. The traveler has the impression more of being in a South American country than in Asia.

Filipinos are considered to be extremely friendly; they are open, warm hearted, and they love to celebrate. The family is very important and the elderly are highly regarded and respected by younger people. Authorities are also held in high regard by the Filipinos; however, it is also expected that the authority figure—for example, the president of a company—looks after the employees in a fatherly manner.

Direct criticism or supporting a contrary opinion meets with disapproval. Every form of exposure, or a situation in which a person is shamed and loses face, must be prevented under all circumstances. Communication is frequently very indirect.

The Web material presents the food business as a friendly and family oriented business that is run by a fatherly president. Also the close ties of the company with Philippine history are highlighted.

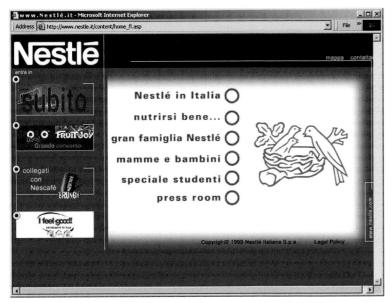

Italians are considered to have a lust for life, to be charming, extremely communicative and talkative. They love good food and good wine. The family plays a big role in Italy and the Italian mother—the *mamme*—has a special significance.

These two topics—family and mother—also appear with special emphasis on the Italian Web pages of NESTLÉ. The design on the start page is kept very elegant and sober; national symbols (such as colors or buildings) do not play a role here.

7.5 Intercultural Web Design Checklist

☐ Do you take specific cultures into consideration with what you have to offer?

☐ Do you provide pages for a specific culture?

☐ To what culture do your users belong?

☐ What values carry great weight for your users?

☐ What symbols reflect the cultural values?

☐ What rituals are typical for the culture?

☐ What heroes does the culture have?

☐ What is the relationship of the individual to the group in the culture?

☐ What preferences are evident?

☐ What colors are especially typical for the culture?

☐ Are you dealing with a linear-active, multi-active, or reactive culture?

☐ How do the people of this culture communicate among themselves?

☐ Do they tend to be talkative or quiet, direct or reserved?

☐ What role do traditions play in the culture? How important are new things in this culture?

☐ How greatly is private life separated from professional life?

☐ What is it about your product (for example, your Web site) that has a relationship to cultural characteristics?

☐ What is it about your product that has a special value for the people of the specific culture?

☐ How could you reach the people of the specific culture?

☐ How can you signal to the people of the culture that you take their culture seriously and hold it in high esteem?

8 Web Accessibility Initiative

This chapter describes the problems that people with visual disabilities have when using the WWW and shows how to design Web pages so that they are accessible.

8.1 The Internet—an Almost Ideal Medium for the Visually Impaired

»The power of the Web is in its universality. Access by everyone regardless of disability is an essential aspect.« Tim Berners-Lee

For people with visual disabilities, the Internet is a fantastic resource for communication and information. For this reason, they use it considerably more intensively than people who are not disabled. In Germany, approximately 80% of disabled people use the Internet, in contrast to the population average of around 50% (at the beginning of 2002). And according to information from the group *Aktion Mensch*, 93% of the disabled Internet experts see »many new opportunities« for themselves in the interactive medium.

Especially **blind people** can now use various assistive technology resources to read Web contents comfortably or to have the contents read to them. One of these possibilities is the *braille line* that is connected to the computer or that is already integrated in the keyboard. It reproduces the text passages of Web pages such that they can be read with the fingertips. However, it is quite expensive, costing around € 8,000. Another possibility is the auditory output of Web text. Screen-reader programs »read« the text aloud, that is, they generate synthesized sounds that are similar to language.

Unfortunately, however, in spite of these assistive technology re-sources, the enjoyment of Web sites for blind people is frequently clouded because almost half of all sites that appear on the Web are not designed to be accessible. Approximately 46% of the content of Web pages cannot be called up by special output devices and approximately 43% of what is offered is difficult to read and navigate (status: spring 2002). In some cases, for reasons of design, text is presented as images without including a description of the content of the image in the ALT tag. Blind people cannot do much with the rollover effects of JavaScript and chic Flash animations because the braille line or the screen reader cannot handle these elements. Also, the use of frames makes orientation difficult and a table poses classification problems.

Of course, we can no longer imagine the Web without these newer technical capabilities, and the point being made here is not to represent Web pages as they looked in the middle of the 1990s: heavy on text, rigid, cluttered, devoid of design elements, and with a gray background. However, with a small effort, it is possible to design Web pages so that they are accessible. You only have to follow a few simple rules.

With the help of a braille line, Web pages can be made readable through the sense of touch. *(Source: F.H. Papenmeier GmbH & Co. KG, www.papenmeier.de)*

For **people with low vision**, there are—in addition to the built-in resources of modern operating systems—special screen magnifiers that make it possible to display portions of the screen content as an enlargement.

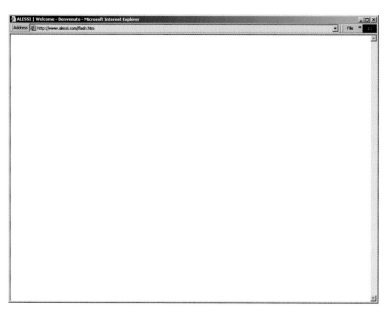

This example uses Flash, but without sound. Now the big guessing game begins for blind people because neither the braille line nor the screen reader can do anything with it.

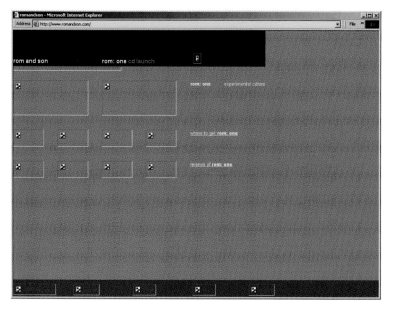

When a blind person uses a screen-reader program to have the Web page shown on the left read aloud, he hears the following: »rom and son * rom colon one cd launch * image image * rom colon one experimental cdrom * image image image image * where to get rom colon one * image image image image * reviews of rom colon one * image: *about romandson* * image: *projects* * image: *clients* * image: *toys* * image: *contact*«

In all probability, the user with the disability will look for another Web site quickly…

»Anyone who slaps a 'this page is best viewed with Browser X' label on a Web page appears to be yearning for the bad old days, before the Web, when you had very little chance of reading a document written on another computer, another word processor, or another network.« Tim Berners-Lee in Technology Review, July 1996

»I'm looking for a bus connection. But I can't read the pocket schedule because I'm blind. So I log on to the Internet. Thanks to modern assistive technology, surfing in the Web is not a problem: the language synthesizer gives an auditory description of the screen content and the braille lines convert the information into the tactile script of raised dots named after the French teacher of the blind, Louis Braille. In this manner, I find the Web site that I'm looking for, but I don't get the schedule information. For those users who can see, the graphics indicate where they should click; but these graphics are not backed with text. And if I simply click anywhere, my 'talking' computer tells me that my text browser does not support the JavaScript application being used. This is not an isolated case. Again and again, I run into Internet offerings that I can't use. Generally they are inaccessible to many other users because they do not function on all machines or they don't take into consideration the various needs and capabilities of the people who visit their site.«
Franz-Josef Hanke, journalist and member of the Committee for a Barrier-Free Internet of the Verein Behinderte in Gesellschaft und Beruf e.V. (BiGuB) (Association for People with Disabilities in Society and Profession)

»I don't use the Internet so much for playing or for entertainment, but as a source of information. And so I am often angered by the whole twaddle with JavaScript or nested frames. A very concrete example is a map in which you have to click if you want to get some information on the vendor's activities in a particular place. Maybe the site looks good, but it excludes blind people and people with other visual disabilities like me from the information. Nevertheless, it is easy to combine attractive Web design and freedom from barriers. No Web designer has to forego fun and games or visual elements. Even a separate text version for blind people and people with other visual disabilities is not necessary if the images are backed by text. We don't want any special treatment. We're concerned about integration.«
Jens Bertrams, board member of the Verein Behinderte in Gesellschaft und Beruf e.V. (BiGuB) (Association for People with Disabilities in Society and Profession)

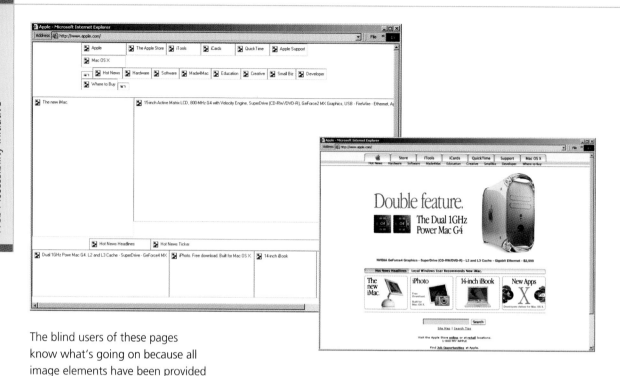

The blind users of these pages
know what's going on because all
image elements have been provided
with text that clearly describes the
content of each image.

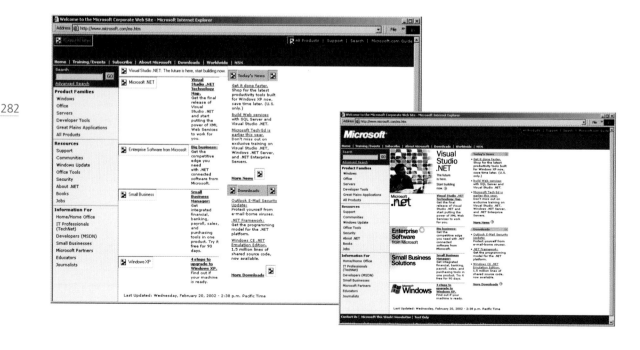

Color Blindness

Approximately 8% of all men and approximately 1% of women are color-blind. While in the case of the very rare complete color blindness (achromatopia) the affected person sees all color tones only as gray values, people with partial color blindness (dichromatism) cannot distinguish clearly the colors red and green from each other. They can orient themselves only by brightness values. Most color-blind people certainly don't see the numeral in the round picture on the right in black and white, but they can no more see the numeral than we do in the gray-scale image. (You will find the color image on the next set of facing pages.)

Color-blind people cannot do very much with an instruction that tells them to click on a red button. They also cannot distinguish words marked in red or green. And a low contrast between foreground and background colors gives them a hard time.

For this reason, use high, **strong contrasts** between foreground and background, between different word distinctions (hot words), and in graphics. For images, always provide an additional description of the picture (ALT tag). If you want to distinguish things by means of color, then please only with the colors blue, yellow, black, and white. Keep in mind, however, that there are other possibilities for emphasis.

To test your pages, make a screen shot and use an image-processing program to convert it to a gray-scale image.

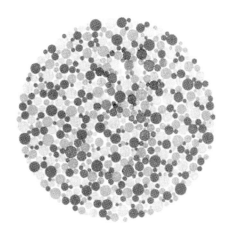

8.2 Guidelines

In 1997, the **World Wide Web Consortium** (W3C) started an initiative for a Web suitable for people with disabilities, the Web Accessibility Initiative (WAI). You can find guidelines, checklists, technical information, and other valuable information on the topic in the information pages of WAI (www.w3.org/WAI).

In the Regulation to Create Barrier-Free Information Technology according to the Law for Equality of People with Disabilities, the **German Parliament** passed a law on July 17, 2002, (www.behindertenbeauftragter.de/files/1027946170.39/RVO-11-BITV.rtf) that is intended to provide barrier-free access to the Internet for people with disabilities as defined by equality. You can find additional pertinent information under http://www.behindertenbeauftragter.de.

On the European level, a »fairer, faster, and more secure Internet« is called for within the framework of the initiative **eEurope 2002**. This initiative also places great importance on the use of the Web by people with disabilities. You can find additional pertinent information under http://europa.eu.int/information_society/eeurope/action_plan/index_en.htm.

The report of the **European Parliament** also supports these endeavors (A5-0147/2002).

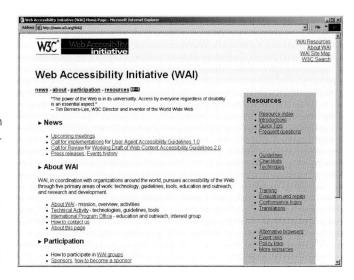

The page Section 508 (www.section508.gov) of the **US federal government** provides information on a law passed in 1998 that stipulates that governmental authorities and institutions design Web offerings that are accessible to people with disabilities. iCan provides help on Section 508 under the URL www.icanonline.net/news/fullpage.cfm/articleid/474A9082-5811-4BC8-938483126A0A6DC3/cx/news.special_reports/article.cfm.

The UNIVERSITY OF WASHING-
TON provides an extensive link list
on the topic of a barrier-free Web
under www.washington.edu/doit/
Resources/web-design.html.

The Trace Research & Development Center of the University of
Wisconsin-Madison provides a collection of useful information under
the title Designing a More Usable
World for All (trace.wisc.edu/
world).

The MICROSOFT CORPORATION
describes its activities with respect
to accessible software and Web
pages under msdn.microsoft.com/
library/default.asp?url=/nhp/Default
.asp?contentid=28000544.

In its Accessibility Cen-
ter (www.3.ibm.com/able/
disability.html), IBM provides a
checklist (www.3.ibm.com/able/
accessweb.html) and more.

Jim Lubin provides extensive informational material on his site
(www.makoa.org/web-design.htm).

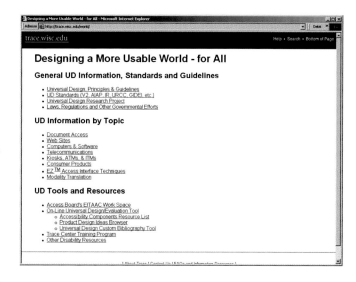

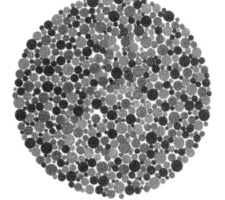

If you do not see the numeral in the
circle to the right, you are red-green
color-blind.

8.3 The Most Important Rules for Accessible Web Pages

Headings

Use the markup possibilities prescribed by HTML that express the logical structure of your text passages. For the headings, use the standard tags <h1> to <h6> and in this way structure things clearly. Displaying headings by means of boldface highlighting or even with a graphic makes it more difficult to understand the document if the user cannot see these features.

Language

In the meta information of the HTML document, enter the natural language that you are using. In this way, you facilitate access.

Text Markup

Use relative text markup such as <strong> and <em> instead of the absolute text formatting <B>. Avoid all rigid formatting such as the <font> tag or similar markup in your HTML files. Indicate the font sizes in no more than relative units. Users must have the capability to adapt text to their special needs.

Hyperlinks

If you use lists of text links (for example, at the bottom of the page), you should place a special character between the links to distinguish them clearly from each other. For example, like this: Start page | Our products | About us | Contacts

In addition, you should always name links clearly with the help of the TITLE attribute by indicating where the link leads. (For example <a href="contact.htm" title="A listing of your contacts with mailing address and telephone number.">)

Structuring

Divide your document clearly with the help of the <div> tag. This measure facilitates understanding of the logical and contextual structure of the contents.

Lists

Always terminate list elements with a period, which indicates to the screen reader the end of the list entry. Numbered list entries are clearer than unnumbered list entries.

Tables

Use tables sparingly because many screen readers read aloud the individual cells of the table; this makes it difficult to perceive a complex table in its totality. Maybe you can also find an alternative here.

The tags <thead> and <tfoot> help you to give the table a logical structure by marking the header and footer areas of the table.

The Summary attribute sums up the contents of the table and should be used in any case. (<table border="1" summary="The following table provides an overview of our auto models.">)

In earlier HTML versions, formatting page areas with the help of tables was the only possible means of designing the screen layout of a Web page to some extent. For people with disabilities, however, tables frequently pose problems. For this reason, design your screen layout with the help of Cascading Style Sheets (CSS), which now can be reproduced correctly by almost all browsers.

Forms

Forms that have to be read aloud or read in braille are, like tables, not necessarily easy to deal with. New tags and attributes in the HTML 4 specification can make life easier. <fieldset> combines elements in forms into groups. The tags <label> and <legend> designate the input fields or selection elements in forms and the particular groups.

Colors

If you use colors to make information understandable, color-blind people or people who have a black-and-white monitor can have a problem. For example, a list of things that one should do or not do should never work with the colors green (for something that one should do) and red (for something that one should not do) because approximately 10% of users cannot distinguish these colors clearly. You should not display differences through colors alone, and pay attention to high contrasts when using colors.

Images

Always mark up images with the ALT tag, which describes the image clearly (<img src="boss.jpg" alt="Our manager">). Applets should also contain a textual description. With the help of the longdesc attribute, you have the capability to refer to an additional page that contains an alternative text concerning the image. If the browser cannot display the graphic, it uses the hyperlink instead. <img src="boss.jpg" alt="Our manager" longdesc="boss.htm">

Image Maps

Marking up each component of the map with an additional description <alt> also applies to image maps. Use client-side image maps and explanatory text for the individual selection possibilities. For server-side maps, provide appropriate text hyperlinks.

Frames

Avoid frames. They pose considerable problems for users with visual disabilities in working with your Web site because the reproduction of frames does not work except in graphic Web browsers. Also, only the start page of frames can be bookmarked, not the individual frameset in the advanced state. Navigation in Web sites with frames is extremely complicated and involved for blind users. However, if you use frames, you should give each HTML file a title that clarifies the function of the file (for example, navigation window).

Pop-Up Windows

Avoid the automatic opening of pop-up windows. They confuse blind users and are also extremely unpopular with other users.

JavaScript and Flash

People with disabilities seldom use JavaScripts and Flash animations. Don't use them, or provide alternatives—pages with Flash and pages with text.

Keyboard Operation

Using the mouse to select is not only a problem for blind people and people with other visual disabilities, but also for people with physical disabilities that do not involve vision. For this reason, it should be possible to use the keyboard to operate hyperlinks or the buttons in forms. This function is handled by the <accesskey> tag, which defines a specific key combination.

Cascading Style Sheets (CSS)

Use Cascading Style Sheets (CSS2) to separate structure and content clearly from each other. This measure facilitates access for blind people to your information and makes it possible to load Web pages more quickly.

8.4 Testing Web Sites

On the Internet, there are many valuable tools for testing Web sites for accessibility. A small selection is presented here.

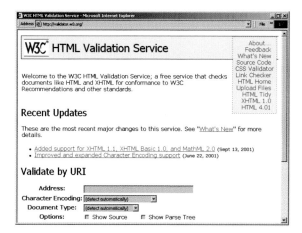

The *Validation Service* of the World Wide Web Consortium (W3C) tests to see if a Web site complies with the W3C standards: validator.w3.org

The Tidy program checks your Web pages and tests to see if your structure is logical and according to standard. www.w3.org/People/Raggett/tidy

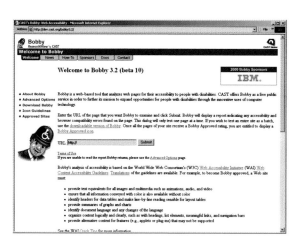

The *Bobby Worldwide* program of the Center for Applied Special Technology of the University of Toronto (CAST) tests Web pages especially to see if they are accessible. www.cast.org/bobby

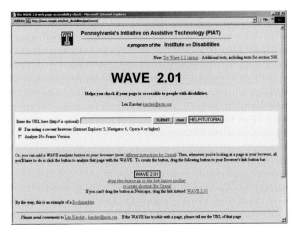

The *WAVE* program (www.temple.edu/inst_disabilities/piat/wave) of Temple University in Philadelphia tests Web sites online.

The *Any Browser Campaign* (www.anybrowser.org) champions Web pages that are independent of specific browser technologies. On its Web site, it provides resources for designing browser-independent HTML documents.

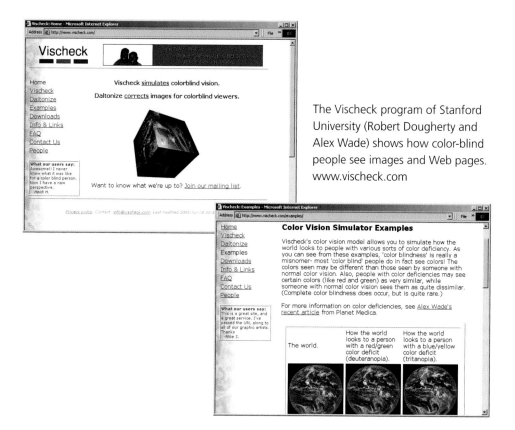

The Vischeck program of Stanford University (Robert Dougherty and Alex Wade) shows how color-blind people see images and Web pages. www.vischeck.com

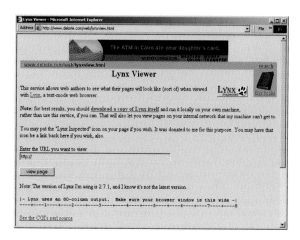

The *Lynx* browser (lynx.browser.org), a text-based Web browser, is a favorite tool for many people with disabilities. The Lynx Viewer (www.delorie.com/web/lynxview.html) displays pages as they would be displayed on Lynx.

DSE—Authoring Environment for Accessible Internet Material

In Germany in the summer of 2002, the Law for Equality of People with Disabilities (Behindertengleichstellungsgesetz, or BGG) was passed, which, among other things, deals with regulations concerning accessible information technology. According to this law, German federal authorities must design their Web sites that are newly developed or revised so that they are accessible, effective immediately. All other Web sites of German federal authorities must be adapted by the year 2005. For private industry, agreements on objectives are to be made with the representatives of associations for people with disabilities.

With the requirement for 'accessibility,' content and technical aspects complement each other. Included here are the following: compatibility with assistive technologies such as screen readers, implementation of alternative operating designs for controlling the mouse, clear design of Web pages, or the availability of a search function with integrated spell checker. The goal is to minimize the mental and physical effort in finding information.

Within the framework of the EU IRIS Project, the Frauenhofer Institute for Applied Information Technology (FIT) is developing the Design Support Environment (DSE)—an authoring environment for accessible Internet material. The intention is to make the development of accessible Web sites easier for Web designers for whom accessibility previously was not a design criterion.

DSE combines recommendations from the Design-for-All-Methods, techniques of user modeling, and guidelines for accessible Web design.

While pages are being created, the program outputs automatic warnings to a certain extent if the guidelines are violated. In addition, training courses and case studies are integrated. These features allow developers and designers to be informed constantly about the consequences of design decisions that they have made and also enable them to display alternatives.

For more information, see: www.fit.fraunhofer.de/projekte/iris.

8.5 Barrier-Free Web Pages Checklist

The World Wide Web Consortium (W3C) has created an extremely helpful checklist for the *Web Content Accessibility Guidelines* which they publish. You can find the original text on this page and those following.

List of Checkpoints for Web Content Accessibility Guidelines 1.0
This version: http://www.w3.org/TR/1999/WAI-WEBCONTENT-19990505/checkpoint-list
(plain text, postscript, pdf)

This document is an appendix to:
http://www.w3.org/TR/1999/WAI-WEBCONTENT-19990505

Latest version of Web Content Accessibility Guidelines 1.0:
http://www.w3.org/TR/WAI-WEBCONTENT

Editors: Wendy Chisholm, Trace R & D Center, University of Wisconsin—Madison; Gregg Vanderheiden, Trace R & D Center, University of Wisconsin—Madison; Ian Jacobs, W3C

Abstract
This document is an appendix to the W3C *Web Content Accessibility Guidelines 1.0*. It provides a list of all checkpoints from the Web Content Accessibility Guidelines 1.0, organized by concept, as a checklist for Web content developers. Please refer to the Guidelines document for introductory information, information about related documents, a glossary of terms, and more.

This list may be used to review a page or site for accessibility. For each checkpoint, indicate whether the checkpoint has been satisfied, has not been satisfied, or is not applicable.

A tabular version of the list of checkpoints is also available (e.g., for printing).

This document has been produced as part of the Web Accessibility Initiative. The goal of the WAI Web Content Guidelines Working Group is discussed in the Working Group charter.

Status of this document

This document is an appendix to a document that has been reviewed by W3C Members and other interested parties and has been endorsed by the Director as a W3C Recommendation. This is a stable document and may be used as reference material or cited as a normative reference from another document. W3C's role in making the Recommendation is to draw attention to the specification and to promote its widespread deployment. This enhances the functionality and universality of the Web.

A list of current W3C Recommendations and other technical documents can be found at http://www.w3.org/TR.

This document has been produced as part of the Web Accessibility Initiative. The goal of the Web Content Guidelines Working Group is discussed in the Working Group charter. Please send comments about this document to wai-wcag-editor@w3.org.

Priorities

Each checkpoint has a priority level assigned by the Working Group based on the checkpoint's impact on accessibility.

[Priority 1]

A Web content developer *must* satisfy this checkpoint. Otherwise, one or more groups will find it impossible to access information in the document. Satisfying this checkpoint is a basic requirement for some groups to be able to use Web documents.

[Priority 2]

A Web content developer *should* satisfy this checkpoint. Otherwise, one or more groups will find it difficult to access information in the document. Satisfying this checkpoint will remove significant barriers to accessing Web documents.

[Priority 3]

A Web content developer *may* address this checkpoint. Otherwise, one or more groups will find it somewhat difficult to access information in the document. Satisfying this checkpoint will improve access to Web documents.

Some checkpoints specify a priority level that may change under certain (indicated) conditions.

Priority 1 checkpoints

In General (Priority 1)

1.1   Provide a text equivalent for every non-text element (e.g., via ALT, LONGDESC, or in element content). This includes: images, graphical representations of text (including symbols), image map regions, animations (e.g., animated GIFs), applets and programmatic objects, ascii art, frames, scripts, images used as list bullets, spacers, graphical buttons, sounds (played with or without user interaction), stand-alone audio files, audio tracks of video, and video.

2.1   Ensure that all information conveyed with color is also available without color, for example from context or markup.

4.1   Clearly identify changes in the natural language of a document's text and any text equivalents (e.g., captions).

6.1   Organize documents so they may be read without style sheets. For example, when an HTML document is rendered without associated style sheets, it must still be possible to read the document.

6.2   Ensure that equivalents for dynamic content are updated when the dynamic content changes.

7.1   Until user agents allow users to control flickering, avoid causing the screen to flicker.

14.1   Use the clearest and simplest language appropriate for a site's content.

And if you use images and image maps (Priority 1)

1.2   Provide redundant text links for each active region of a server-side image map.

9.1   Provide client-side image maps instead of server-side image maps except where the regions cannot be defined with an available geometric shape.

And if you use tables (Priority 1)

5.1   For data tables, identify row and column headers.

5.2 For data tables that have two or more logical levels of row or column headers, use markup to associate data cells and header cells.

And if you use frames (Priority 1)
12.1 Title each frame to facilitate frame identification and navigation.

And if you use applets and scripts (Priority 1)
6.3 Ensure that pages are usable when scripts, applets, or other programmatic objects are turned off or not supported. If this is not possible, provide equivalent information on an alternative accessible page.

And if you use multimedia (Priority 1)
1.3 Until user agents can automatically read aloud the text equivalent of a visual track, provide an auditory description of the important information of the visual track of a multimedia presentation.

1.4 For any time-based multimedia presentation (e.g., a movie or animation), synchronize equivalent alternatives (e.g., captions or auditory descriptions of the visual track) with the presentation.

And if all else fails (Priority 1)
11.4 If, after best efforts, you cannot create an accessible page, provide a link to an alternative page that uses W3C technologies, is accessible, has equivalent information (or functionality), and is updated as often as the inaccessible (original) page.

Priority 2 checkpoints
In General (Priority 2)
2.2 Ensure that foreground and background color combinations provide sufficient contrast when viewed by someone having color deficits or when viewed on a black and white screen. [Priority 2 for images, Priority 3 for text].

3.1 When an appropriate markup language exists, use markup rather than images to convey information.

3.2   Create documents that validate to published formal grammars.

3.3   Use style sheets to control layout and presentation.

3.4   Use relative rather than absolute units in markup language attribute values and style sheet property values.

3.5   Use header elements to convey document structure and use them according to specification.

3.6   Mark up lists and list items properly.

3.7   Mark up quotations. Do not use quotation markup for formatting effects such as indentation.

6.5   Ensure that dynamic content is accessible or provide an alternative presentation or page.

7.2   Until user agents allow users to control blinking, avoid causing content to blink (i.e., change presentation at a regular rate, such as turning on and off).

7.4   Until user agents provide the ability to stop the refresh, do not create periodically auto-refreshing pages.

7.5   Until user agents provide the ability to stop auto-redirect, do not use markup to redirect pages automatically. Instead, configure the server to perform redirects.

10.1   Until user agents allow users to turn off spawned windows, do not cause pop-ups or other windows to appear and do not change the current window without informing the user.

11.1   Use W3C technologies when they are available and appropriate for a task and use the latest versions when supported.

11.2   Avoid deprecated features of W3C technologies.

12.3   Divide large blocks of information into more manageable groups where natural and appropriate.

13.1   Clearly identify the target of each link.

13.2   Provide metadata to add semantic information to pages and sites.

13.3   Provide information about the general layout of a site (e.g., a site map or table of contents).

13.4   Use navigation mechanisms in a consistent manner.

And if you use tables (Priority 2)

5.3   Do not use tables for layout unless the table makes sense when linearized. Otherwise, if the table does not make sense, provide an alternative equivalent (which may be a linearized version).

5.4   If a table is used for layout, do not use any structural markup for the purpose of visual formatting.

And if you use frames (Priority 2)

12.2   Describe the purpose of frames and how frames relate to each other if it is not obvious by frame titles alone.

And if you use forms (Priority 2)

10.2   Until user agents support explicit associations between labels and form controls, for all form controls with implicitly associated labels, ensure that the label is properly positioned.

12.4   Associate labels explicitly with their controls.

And if you use applets and scripts (Priority 2)

6.4   For scripts and applets, ensure that event handlers are input device-independent.

7.3   Until user agents allow users to freeze moving content, avoid movement in pages.

8.1   Make programmatic elements such as scripts and applets directly accessible or compatible with assistive technologies [Priority 1 if functionality is important and not presented elsewhere, otherwise Priority 2.]

9.2   Ensure that any element that has its own interface can be operated in a device-independent manner.

9.3   For scripts, specify logical event handlers rather than device-dependent event handlers.

Priority 3 checkpoints
In General (Priority 3)
4.2   Specify the expansion of each abbreviation or acronym in a document where it first occurs.

4.3   Identify the primary natural language of a document.

9.4   Create a logical tab order through links, form controls, and objects.

9.5   Provide keyboard shortcuts to important links (including those in client-side image maps), form controls, and groups of form controls.

10.5 Until user agents (including assistive technologies) render adjacent links distinctly, include non-link, printable characters (surrounded by spaces) between adjacent links.

11.3 Provide information so that users may receive documents according to their preferences (e.g., language, content type, etc.)

13.5 Provide navigation bars to highlight and give access to the navigation mechanism.

13.6 Group related links, identify the group (for user agents), and, until user agents do so, provide a way to bypass the group.

13.7 If search functions are provided, enable different types of searches for different skill levels and preferences.

13.8 Place distinguishing information at the beginning of headings, paragraphs, lists, etc.

13.9   Provide information about document collections (i.e., documents comprising multiple pages.).

13.10 Provide a means to skip over multi-line ASCII art.

14.2   Supplement text with graphic or auditory presentations where they will facilitate comprehension of the page.

14.3   Create a style of presentation that is consistent across pages.

And if you use images and image maps (Priority 3)
1.5   Until user agents render text equivalents for client-side image map links, provide redundant text links for each active region of a client-side image map.

And if you use tables (Priority 3)
5.5   Provide summaries for tables.

5.6   Provide abbreviations for header labels.

10.3   Until user agents (including assistive technologies) render side-by-side text correctly, provide a linear text alternative (on the current page or some other) for *all* tables that lay out text in parallel, word-wrapped columns.

And if you use forms (Priority 3)
10.4   Until user agents handle empty controls correctly, include default, place-holding characters in edit boxes and text areas.

9
Appendix

The appendix provides references to related literature for further reading and an overview of the sources used.

9.1 References

General Information

Alexander, Christopher W. (1970): Notes on the Synthesis of Form. Cambridge, MA: Harvard University Press

Beyer, Hugh / Holzblatt, Karen (1998): Contextual Design. San Francisco, CA: Morgan Kaufmann Publishers

Bickford, P. (1997): Interface Design. The Art of Developing Easy-to-Use Software. Chestnut Hill, MA: Academic Press

Black, Roger (1997): Web Sites that work. San Jose: Adobe Press

Bonsiepe, Gui (1999): Interface an Approach to Design. Maastricht: Jan Van Eyck Akad.

Brinck, Tom / Gergle, Darren / Wood, Scott D. (2001): Usability for the Web: Designing Web Sites that Work. San Francisco, CA: Morgan Kaufmann Publishers

Brown, C. M. (1988): Human-Computer Interface Design Guidelines. Norwood, NJ: Ablex

Card, S. / Moran, T. / Newell, A. (1983): The Psychology of Human Computer Interaction. Hillsdale, NJ: Lawrence Erlbaum Associates

Cato, John (2001): User-Centered Web Design. Reading, MA: Addison-Wesley

Coe, Marlana (1996): Human Factors for Technical Communication. New York et al.: John Wiley & Sons

Cooper, Alan (1995): About Face. The Essentials of User Interface Design. Foster City, CA: IDG Books

Dayton, T. / McFarland, A. / Kramer, J. (1998): Bridging User Needs to Object Oriented GUI Prototype via Task Object Design. In: Wood, L. (ed.): User Interface Design. Bridging the Gap from Requirements to Design. Boca Raton: FL: CRC Press, 15–56

Eysenck, Michael W. / Keane, Michael W. (1990): Cognitive Psychology. A student´s handbook. Hillsdale, NJ

Flanders, V. / Willis, M. (1998): Web Pages That Suck. Learning Good Design by Looking at Bad Design. San Francisco, CA: Sybex

Fowler, S. (1998): GUI Design Handbook. New York: McGraw-Hill

Galitz, Wilbert O. (1989): Handbook of Screen Format Design. 3rd edition, QED Information Sciences Inc.

Gentner, D. / Grudin, J. (1990): Why Good Engineers (Sometimes) Create Bad Interfaces. In: Proceedings of the ACM Conference on Computer-Human Interaction (CHI ´90), 277–282

Goto, Kelly / Cotler, Emily (2001): Web Redesign: Workflow That Works. Indianapolis, IN: New Riders Publishing

Heckel, Paul (1994): The Elements of Friendly Software Design. London: Sybex

Johnson, Jeff (2000): GUI Bloopers Don´ts and Do´s for Software Development and Web Designers. San Francisco, CA: Morgan Kaufmann Publishers

Johnson, Jeff / Beach, R. (1988): Styles in Document Editing Systems. In: IEEE Computers 21 (1), 32–43

Kraut, R. (ed.) (1996): The Internet @ Home. In: Special Section of Communications of the ACM 39 (12), 33–74

Krug, Steve (2000): Don´t Make Me Think. A Common Sense Approach to Web Usability. Indianapolis, IN: New Riders Publishing

Landauer, T. K. (1995): The Trouble with Computers Usefulness, Usability, and Productivity. Cambridge, MA: MIT Press

Laurel, Brenda (ed.) (1990): The Art of Human-Computer Interface Design. Reading, MA: Addison-Wesley

Lopuck, Lisa (1996): Designing Multimedia. Berkeley, CA: Peachpit Press

Mandel, T. (1997): The Elements of User Interface Design. New York: John Wiley & Sons

Marcus, Aaron (1994): Graphic Design for Usable User Interface. In: ACM Siggraph 94 Course Notes #20. Emeryville, CA, 6 ff.

McFarland, A. / Dayton, T. (1995): Design Guide for Multiplatform Graphical User Interfaces. Issue 3, LPR 13. Piscataway, NJ: Bellcore

McKelvey, Roy (1998): Hypergraphics. Hove, UK: Rotovision

Mullet, K. / Sano, D. (1995): Designing Visual Interfaces. Mountain View, CA: Sunsoft Press

Nielsen, Jakob (1993): Usability Engineering. San Diego, CA: Academic Press

Nielsen, Jakob (1996): The Top Ten Mistakes of Web Design. [http://www.useit.com/alertbox/9605.html]

Nielsen, Jakob (1999a): Designing Web Usability. The Practice of Simplicity. Indianapolis, IN: New Riders Publishing

Nielsen, Jakob (1999b): Differences Between Print Design and Web Design. [http://www.useit.com/alertbox/990124.html]

Nielsen, Jakob (1999c): »Top Ten Mistakes« Revisited (Alertbox May 1999). [http://www.useit.com/alertbox/990502.html]

Nielsen, Jakob (1999d): Top-10 New Mistakes of Web Design (Alertbox May 1999). [http://www.useit.com/alertbox/990530.html]

Nielsen, Jakob / Tahir, Marie (2002): Homepage Usability. 50 Websites Deconstructed. Indianapolis, IN: New Riders Publishing

Norman, Donald A. (1988): The Psychology of Everyday Things. New York: Basic Books/Harper Collins

Norman, Donald A. (1990): The Design of Everyday Things. New York: Double day Books

Norman, Donald A. (1994): Things That Make Us Smart. Defending Human Attributes in the Age of the Machine. Cambridge, MA: Perseus Publishing

Norman, Donald A. (1999): The Invisible Computer. Why Good Products Can Fail, the Personal Computer Is So Complex and Information Aplliances Are The Solution. Cambridge, MA: MIT Press

Preece, J. et al. (1994): Human-computer interaction. Wokingham: Addison-Wesley

Raskin, Jef (2000): The Humane Interface. Reading, MA: Addison-Wesley

Reeves, Byron / Nass, Clifford (1996): The Media Equation. How People Treat Computers, Television, and New Media Like Real People and Places. Cambridge: Cambridge University Press

Rosdale, Ray M. (Hrsg.) (1999): Erfolgreiches Web-Design. München: Humbold Taschenbuchverlag

Schuler, D. / Namioka, A. (1993): Participatory Design. Principles and Practices Hillsdale, NJ: Lawrence Erlbaum Associates

Schuler, W. / Hannemann, J. / Streitz, N. (eds.) (1995): Designing user interfaces for hypermedia. Berlin: Springer-Verlag

Schulz, Angelika (1998): Interfacedesign. Die visuelle Gestaltung interaktiver Computeranwendungen. St. Ingbert: Röhrig

Shneiderman, Ben (1997): Designing the User Interface. Strategies for Effective Human-Computer Interaction. Reading, MA: Addison-Wesley

Siegel, David (1998): Web Site Design. 2. Aufl., München: Markt + Technik

Sutcliffe, Alistair / Ziegler, Jürgen / Johnson, Peter (1998): Designing Effective and Usable Multimedia Systems. Boston: Kluwer Academic Publishers

Tullis, Thomas S. (1988): Screen Design. In: Helander, Marc (ed.): Handbook of Human-Computer Interaction. North Holland: Morgan Kaufmann

Veen, Jeffrey (2000): The Art and Science of Web Design. Indianapolis, IN: New Riders Publishing

Wandmacher, Jens (1993): Software-Ergonomie. Berlin, New York: de Gruyter

Weinman, Lynda (1998): Deconstructing Webdesign. München: Markt + Technik

Weinman, Lynda (1998): WebDesign. Zürich: Midas

Weinshenk, S. / Jamar, P. / Yeo, S. (1997): GUI Design Essentials. New York: John Wiley & Sons

Weizenbaum, Joseph (1976): Computer Power and Human Reason. San Francisco, CA: W.H. Freeman

Weizenbaum, Joseph (1966): ELIZA—A Computer Program for the Study of Natural Language Communication between Man and Machine. In: Communications of the ACM 9, 36–45

Williams, Robin / Tollett, John (2000a): Robin Williams Design Workshop. Berkeley, CA: Peachpit Press

Williams, Robin / Tollett, John (2000b): The Non-Designer's Web Book. 2nd edition, Berkeley, CA: Peachpit Press

Williams, Robin / Tollett, John / Rohr, Dave / Rohr, David (2001): Robin Williams Web Design Workshop. Berkeley, CA: Peachpit Press

Wilson, Stephen (1996): World Wide Web Design Guide. München: Markt + Technik

Zeldman, Jeffrey (2001): Taking Your Talent to the Web: Making the Transition from Graphic Design to Web Design. Indianapolis, IN: New Riders Publishing

Accessible Web

Clark, Joe (2002): Building Accessible Websites. Indianapolis, IN: New Riders Publishing

Cook, Albert M. / Hussey, Susan M. (2001): Assistive Technologies: Principles and Practice. 2nd edition, Mosby-Year Book

IBM: Accessibility Center [http://www-3.ibm.com/able]

King, Thomas W. (1998): Assistive Technology: Essential Human Factors. Boston: Allyn & Bacon

Mates, Barbara T. / Wakefield, Doug / Dixon, Judith M. (2000): Adaptive Technology for the Internet: Making Electronic Resources Accessible to All. Chicago, IL: American Library Assn Editions

Microsoft: Accessibility. Technology for Everyone [http://www.microsoft.com/enable]

Moulton, Gary / Huyler, LaDeana / Hertz, Janice / Levenson, Mark (2002): Accessible Technology in Today's Business. Microsoft Press

Paciello, Michael G. / Paciello, Mike (2000): Web Accessibility for People with Disabilities. Sacramento, CA: CMP Books

Scherer, Marcia J. (2000): Living in the State of Stuck: How Assistive Technology Impacts the Lives of People with Disabilities. 3rd edition, Cambridge, MA: Brookline Books

Thatcher, Jim / Waddell, Cynthia / Henry, Schawn / Swierenga, Sarah / Urban, Mark / Burks, Michael / Regan, Bob / Bohman, Paul (2002): Constructing Accessible Web Sites. Waltham, MA: Glasshouse Publ.

trace.wisc.edu: Java Accessibility and Usability Work [http://trace.wisc.edu/world/java/java.htm]

US Department of Justice: Web Site Accessibility Questionnaire for Component Web Contacts [http://www.usdoj.gov/crt/508/web.htm]

W3C: Accessibility Features of SMIL [http://www.w3.org/TR/SMIL-access]

Agents

Intelligent Agents Project at IBM T. J. Watson Research [http://www.research.ibm.com/iagents]

Software Agents Group des MIT Media Lab [http://www.media.mit.edu/research/group.php?type=researchGroup&id=4]

Color

Agoston, George A. (1987): Color theory and its application in art and design. New York: Springer-Verlag

Albers, Josef (1987): Interaction of Color. Yale University Press

Birren, Faber (1984): Color & Human Response: Aspects of Light and Color Bearing on the Reactions of Living Things and the Welfare of Human Beings. New York: John Wiley & Sons

Birren, Faber (ed.) (1987): The Principles of Harmony and Contrast of Colors and Their Applications to the Arts. Schiffer Publishing

Birren, Faber (2000): The Symbolism of Color. Secancus, NJ: Citadel Press

Coe, Marlana (1996): Human Factors for Technical Communicators. New York: John Wiley & Sons

Durrett, H. John (1997): Color and the Computer. New York: Academic Press

Favre, Jean-Paul / November, André (1979): Color and Communication. Zürich

Fehrman, Cherie / Fehrman, Kenneth R. (1999): Color: The Secret Influence. Upper Saddle River, NJ: Prentice Hall

Gage, John (1999): Color and Culture: Practice and Meaning from Antiquity to Abstraction. University of California Press

Gage, John (2000): Color and Meaning: Art, Science, and Symbolism. University of California Press

Hope, Augustine / Walch, Margaret (1990): The Color Compendium. Van Nostrand Reinhold

Itten, Johannes (1986): The Color Star. New York: John Wiley & Sons

Itten, Johannes (1997): The Art of Color: The Subjective Experience and Objective Rationale of Color. New York: John Wiley & Sons

Mahnke, Frank H. / Mahnke, Rudolf H. (1996): Color, Environment, and Human Response. New York: John Wiley & Sons

Pile, John F. (1997): Color in Interior Design. New York: McGraw-Hill

Pring, Roger (2000): www.Color. New York: Watson-Guptill Publications

Thorell, Lisa G. / Smith, Wanda J. (1990): Using Computer Color Effectively. An Illustrated Reference. Upper Saddle River: NJ: Prentice Hall

Tufte, Edward (1990): Envisioning Information. Cheshire, CT: Graphics Press

Whelan, Bride M. (1994): Color Harmony 2. A Guide to Creative Color Combinations. Gloucester, MA: Rockport

Wong, Wucius (1997): Principles of Form and Design. New York: John Wiley & Sons

306

Communication

Bateson, Gregory (2000): Steps to an Ecology of Mind: Collected Essays in Anthropology, Psychiatry, Evolution, and Epistemology. Chicago, IL: University of Chicago Press

Watzlawick, Paul (1967): Pragmatics of Human Communication: A Study of Interactional Patterns, Pathologies, and Paradoxes. New York: W W Norton & Company

Emotion / Motivation

Carter, Rita (2000): Mapping the Mind. University of California Press

Cooper, John M. (1998): Reason and Emotion. Princeton University Press

Cornelius, Randolph R. (1995): The Science of Emotion. Research and Tradition in the Psychology of Emotion. Upper Saddle River, NJ: Prentice Hall

Damasio, Antonio R. (1995): Descartes' Error: Emotion, Reason, and the Human Brain. Avon Books

Damasio, Antonio R. (1999): The Feeling of What Happens: Body and Emotion in the Making of Consciousness. Orlando, FL: Harcourt

Edwards, D. C. (1998). Motivation and Emotion. London: Sage Publications

Ekman, Paul / Davidson, Richard J. (eds.) (1995): The Nature of Emotion: Fundamental Questions. Oxford University Press

Felser, Georg (1997): Werbe- und Konsumentenpsychologie. Eine Einführung. Heidelberg: Spektrum Akademischer Verlag

Goleman, Daniel (1997): Emotional Intelligence. Bantam Dell Publishing Group

Goleman, Daniel (2000): Working With Emotional Intelligence. Bantam Dell Publishing Group

Herzberg, Frederick / Mausner, Bernard / Snyderman, Barbara Bloch (1993): The Motivation to Work. Somerset, NJ: Transaction Publ.

Izard, Carrol E. (1977): Human Emotions. New York: Plenum Press

Jenkins, J. M. / Oatley, K. / Stein, N. (1995): Understanding Emotions. Oxford: Blackwell

Lane, Richard D. / Nadel, Lynn / Ahern, Geoffrey (eds.) (2000): Cognitive Neuroscience of Emotion. Oxford University Press

Ledoux, Joseph (1998): The Emotional Brain: The Mysterious Underpinnings of Emotional Life. Camichael, CA: Touchstone Books

Lewis, Michael / Haviland-Jones, Jannette (eds.) (2000): Handbook of Emotions. 2nd edition, New York: Guilford Press

Maslow, Abraham Harold / Frager, Robert / Fadiman, James (1987): Motivation and Personality. Reading, MA: Addison-Wesley

Mayne, Tracy J. / Bonanno, Georg A. / Scherer, Klaus (eds.) (2001): Emotions. New York: Guilford Press

McCelland, David (1988): Human Motivation. Cambridge University Press

Munro, D. / Schumaker, J. F. / Carr, S. C. (1997): Motivation and Culture. London: Routledge

Murray, Edward J. (1964): Motivation and Emotion. Upper Saddle River, NJ: Prentice Hall

Panksepp, Jaak: Affective Neuroscience (1998): The Foundations of Human and Animal Emotions. Oxford University Press

Petri, Herbert L. (1995): Motivation: Theory, Research, and Applications. Belmont, CA: Wadsworth

Picard, Rosalind W. (2000): Affective Computing. Cambridge, MA: MIT Press

Picard, Rosalind W.: Affective Computing [http://affect.media.mit.edu]

Power, M. / Dalgleish, T. (1997): Cognition and Emotion. Hove, UK: The Psychology Press

Reeve, Johnmarshall (2000): Understanding Motivation and Emotion. Hoboken, NJ: John Wiley & Sons

Reeves, Byron / Nass, Clifford (1996): The Media Equation. How People Treat Computers, Television, and New Media Like Real People and Places. Cambridge: Cambridge University Press

Rolls, Edmund T. (1999): The Brain and Emotion. Oxford University Press

Sansone, Carol / Harackiewicz, Judith M. (eds.) (2000): Intrinsic and Extrinsic Motivation: The Search for Optimal Motivation and Performance. San Diego, CA: Academic Press

Scherer, Klaus R. (1988): Facets of Emotion. Hillsdale, NJ: Lawrence Erlbaum Associates

Weiner, B. (1996): Human Motivation. London: Sage Publications

Weizenbaum, Joseph (1976): Computer power and human reason: from judgment to calculation. New York: W H Freeman & Co

Flash

Macromedia: Usability/User-Centered Design. [http://www.macromedia.com/desdev/topics/usability.html]

MacGregor, Chris / Waters, Crystal / Doull, David (2002): The Flash Usability Guide: Interacting with Flash MX. Friends of ED

MacGregor, Chris (o.J.): Developing User-Friendly Macromedia Flash Content. [http://www.macromedia.com/software/flash/productinfo/usability/whitepapers/usability_flazoom.pdf]

MacGregor, Chris: Flazoom.com [http://www.flazoom.com]

Nielsen, Jakob (2000a): Flash: 99% Bad. Jakob Nielsen's Alertbox, October 29, 2000 [http://www.useit.com/alertbox/20001029.html]

Perfetti, Christine (2002): Flash Strikes Back: Creating Powerful Web Applications [http://www.uie.com/Articles/flash_strikes_back.htm]

Schroeder, Will / Perfetti, Christine / Spool, Jared M. (2002): Enhancing User Interaction in Pet Market. [http://www.macromedia.com/desdev/mx/blueprint/articles/enhancing_interaction.pdf]

Gestalt Laws

Arnheim, Rudolf (1983): Art and Visual Perception: A Psychology of the Creative Eye. University of California Press

Arnheim, Rudolf (1989): Visual Thinking. University of California Press

Card, S. K. / Robertson, G. G. / Mackinlay, J. D. (1991): The information visualizer: An information workspace. In: Proceedings of the ACM CHI'91 Conference (New Orleans, LA, 28 April–2 May), 181–188

Ellis, Willis D. / Koffka, K. (1999): A Source Book of Gestalt Psychology. London, New York: Routledge

Koffka, K. (1967): Principles of Gestalt Psychology. London: Routledge

Kohler, Wolfgang (1992): Gestalt Psychology: An Introduction to New Concepts in Modern Psychology. New York: Liveright

Shneiderman, B. (1982): Designing Computer System Messages. In: Communications of the ACM 25 (9), 610–611

Shneiderman, B. (1984): Response Time and Display Rate in Human Performance with Computers. In: ACM Computing Surveys 16 (4), 265–285

Zakia, Richard D. (1997): Perception and Imaging. Oxford: Butterworth-Heinemann

Hypertext

Bush, Vannevar (1945): As We May Think. In: Atlantic Monthly 176, 1, 1945, 101–103 [http://www.theatlantic.com/unbound/flashbks/computer/bushf.htm]

Conclin, J. (1987): Hypertext. An Introduction and Survey. In: Computer, 20 (9), 1987, 17–41

Dillon, A. / McKnight, C. / Richardson, J. (eds.) (1993): Hypertext—a psychological perspective. Chichester: Ellis Horwood Ltd

Gall, J. E. / Hannafin, M. J. (1994): A Framework for the Study of Hypertext. In: Instructional Science, 22, 1994, 207–232

Landow, George P. (ed.) (1994): Hyper/Text/Theory. Baltimore: John Hopkins University Press

Nielsen, Jakob (1989): The matters that really matter for hypertext usability. In: Proc. ACM Hypertext '89 Conf. (Pittsburgh, PA, 5-8 Nov.), 23–248

Nyce, J. M. / Kahn, P. D. (eds.) (1991): Memex to Hypertext. Vannevar Bush and the Mind's Machine. San Diego, CA: Academic Press

Potosnak, K. M. / Hayes, P. J. / Rosson, M. B. / Schneider, M. L. / Whiteside, J. A. (1986): Classifying users: A hard look at some controversial issues. In: Proc. ACM CHI'86 Conf. (Boston, MA, 13–17 April), 84–88

Project Xanadu® [http://xanadu.com]

Shneiderman, B. / Kearsley, G. (1989): Hypertext Hands-On! An Introduction to a New Way of Organizing and Accessing Information. Reading, MA: Addison-Wesley

Icons

Caplin, Steve (2001): Icon Design: Graphic Icons in Computer Interface Design. New York: Watson-Guptill Publications

Horton, William (1994): The Icon Book. Visual Symbols for Computer Systems and Documentation. New York: John Wiley & Sons

Thomas, Gregory / Powell, Earl A. (2000): How to Design Logos, Symbols & Icons: 23 Internationally Renowned Studios Reveal How They Develop Trademarks for Print and New Media. North Light Books

Information Design

Card, S. / Gershon, N. / Eick, S. G. (1998): Information visualisation. In: Interactions, Vol. 5, No. 2

Jacobson, Robert (ed.) (1999): Information Design. Cambridge, MA: MIT Press

Tufte, Edward R. (1990): Envisioning Information. Cheshire, CT: Graphics Press

Interaction

Badre, Albert N. (2002): Shaping Web Usability: Interaction Design in Context. Reading, MA: Addison-Wesley

Baecker, Ronald M. / Grudig, Jonathan / Buxton, William / Greenberg, Saul (1995): Readings in Human-Computer Interaction: Toward the Year 2000. San Francisco, CA: Morgan Kaufmann Publishers

Baggerman, Lisa (2000): Design for Interaction. Gloucester, MA: Rockport Publishers

Barber, R. / Lucas, H. (1983): System Response Time, Operator Productivity, and Job Satisfaction. In: Communications of the ACM, 11, 972–986

Borchers, Jan (2001): A Pattern Approach to Interaction Design. New York: John Wiley & Sons

Card, Stuart K. / Moran, Thomas P. / Newell, Allen (1983): The Psychology of Human-Computer Interaction. Hillsdale, NJ: Lawrence Erlbaum Assoc

Card, Stuart K. / Robertson, G. G. / Mackinlay, J. D. (1991): The information visualizer: An information workspace. In: Proc. ACM CHI"91 Conf. (New Orleans, LA, 28 April – 2 May), 181–188

Carroll, John M. (2001): Human-Computer Interaction in the New Millennium. Reading, MA: Addison-Wesley

Dix, Alan J. / Finlay, Janet E. / Abowd, Gregory D. / Beale, Russell (1998): Human Computer Interaction. 2nd edition, Upper Saddle River, NJ: Prentice Hall

Draper, Stephen / Norman, Donald A. (1986): User Centered System Design: New Perspectives on Human-Computer Interaction. Hillsdale, NJ: Lawrence Erlbaum Assoc

Edwards, E. / Lees, F. (eds.) (1974): The Human Operator in Process Control. London: Taylor & Francis Ltd.

Faulkner, Christine (1997): The Essence of Human-Computer Interaction. Upper Saddle River, NJ: Prentice Hall

Fitts, P. M. (1954): The Information Capacity of the Human Motor System in Controlling the Amplitude of Movement. Journal of Experimental Psychology 47, 381–391

Hackos, JoAnn T. / Redish, Janice C. (1998): User and Task Analysis for Interface Design. New York: John Wiley & Sons

Helander, Martin (ed.) (1998): Handbook of Human-Computer Interaction. New York: North-Holland

Jones, Mark K. (1989): Human Computer Interaction: A Design Guide. London: Sage Publications

MacAulay, L. (1994): Human Computer Interaction for Software Design. London et al.: Chapman & Hall

MacGregor, Chris (2000): Make Sure Usability 'Fitts' Flash. [http://www.flazoom.com/news/fitts_07102000.shtml]

Miller, R. B. (1968): Response time in man-computer conversational transactions. In: Proc. AFIPS Spring Joint Computer Conference. Vol. 33, 267–277

Ntuen, Celestine A. (ed.) (1996): Human Interaction With Complex Systems: Conceptual Principles and Design Practice. Dordrecht et al.: Kluwer Academic Publishers

Preece, Jennifer / Rogers, Yvonne / Sharp, Helen (2002): Beyond Interaction Design. New York: John Wiley & Sons

Preece, Jennifer / Rogers, Yvonne / Sharp, Helen (2002): Interaction Design. New York: John Wiley & Sons

Preece, Jennifer / Rogers, Yvonne / Sharp, Helen / Beyond, David (1994): Human-Computer Interaction. Reading, MA: Addison-Wesley

Raskin, Jef (2000): The Humane Interface: New Directions for Designing Interactive Systems. Reading, MA: Addison-Wesley

Rosson, Mary Beth / Carroll, John M. / Cerra, Diane D. (eds.) (2001): Usability Engineering: Scenario-Based Development. San Francisco, CA: Morgan Kaufmann Publishers

Shneiderman, B. (1982): Designing computer system messages. In: Communications of ACM 25, 9 (Sept.), 610–611

Thadhani, A. (1981): Interactive User Productivity. In: IBM Systems Journal 20 (4), 407–423

Tognazzini, Bruce (1999): A Quiz Designed to Give You Fitts [http://www.flazoom.com/news/fitts_07102000.shtml]

Welford, A. T. (1980): Reaction Time. New York: Academic Press

Woodson, W. E. (1981): Human Factors Design Handbook. New York: McGraw-Hill

Intercultural Design

Axtell, Roger E. (ed.) (1985): Does and Taboos Around the World. Hoboken NJ: John Wiley & Sons

Barlett, Christopher A. / Ghoshal, Sumantra (1990): Managing across Borders The Transnational Solution. Boston: Harvard Business School Press

Berry, Michael (1992): Know Theyself and the Other Fellow Too: Strategies for Effective Cross-Cultural Communication. Ithaka, NY: Institute for European Studies

Bohm, David (1996): On Dialogue. London: Routledge

Bremer, Katharina / Roberts, Celia / Vasseur, M. T. (Contributor) / Simonot, Margaret (Contributor) (1996): Achieving Understanding: Discourse in Intercultural Encounters. London: Longman

Chen, Guo-Ming / Starosta, William J. (1997): Foundations of Intercultural Communication. Boston, MA: Allyn & Bacon

Condon, John C. / Yousef, Fathi (1975): An Introduction to Intercultural Communication. New York: Macmillan

Elashmawi, Farid / Harris, Philip R. (1993): Multicultural Management: New Skills for Global Success. Houston: Gulf Publishing

Fisher, Glen (1980): International Negotiation: A Cross-Cultural Perspective. Yarmouth, ME: Intercultural Press

Furnham, Adrian / Bochner, Stephen (1986): Culture Shock: Psychological Reactions to Unfamiliar Environments. London: Methuen

Hall, Edward Twitchell (1977): Beyond Culture. Garden City, NY: Anchor

Hall, Edward Twitchell (1990): The Hidden Dimension. Garden City, NY: Anchor

Hall, Edward Twitchell / Reed Hall, Mildred (1990): Understanding Cultural Differentes: Germans, French and Americans. Yarmouth, ME: Intercultural Press

Hampden-Turner, Charles / Trompenaars, Fons (1993): The Seven Cultures of Capitalism: Value systems for Creating Wealth in the United States, Britain, Japan, Germany, France, Sweden and The Netherlands. New York: Doubleday

Harris, Philip R. / Moran, Robert T. (1979): Managing Cultural Differentes: High-Performance Strategies for Today's Global Manager. Houston: Gulf Publishing

Hendry, Joy (1993): Wrapping Culture: Politeness, Presentation, and Power in Japan and Other Societies. Oxford: Clarendon Press

Hofstede, Geert (1980): Culture's Consequences: International Differentes in Work-Related Values. London: Sage Publications

Hofstede, Geert (1996): Cultures and Organizations. New York: McGraw-Hill

Hofstede, Geert (2001a): Culture's Consequences: Comparing Values, Behaviors, Institutions, and Organizations Across Nations. 2nd edition, London: Sage Publications

Hogan-Garcia, Mikel (1998): Four Skills of Cultural Diversity Competence: A Process for Understanding and Practice. Belmont, CA: Wadsworth

Holden, Nigel J. (1992): Management, Language and Eurocommunication, 1992 and Beyond. Ithaka, NY: Institute for European Studies

Kealey, Daniel J. (1989): A Study of Cross-Cultural Effectiveness. In: International Journal of Intercultural Relations 13, No. 3 (1989), 387–395

Landis, Dan / Bhagat, Rabi S. (eds.) (1996): Handbook of Intercultural Training. London: Sage Publications

Levine, Robert (1997): A Geography of Time. New York: Basic Books / Harper Collins

Lewis, Richard D. (1999): When Cultures Collide. London: Nicolas Brealey

Lustig, Myron W. / Koester, Jolene (2002): Intercultural Competence: Interpersonal Communication Across Cultures. 4th edition, Boston, MA: Allyn & Bacon

Martin, Judith N. (ed.) (1989): Intercultural Communication Competence. International Journal of Intercultural Relations 13, No. 3

Martin, Judith N. / Nakayama, Thomas K. (1999): Intercultural Communication in Contexts. New York: WCB/McGraw-Hill

Mole, John (1995): Mind Your Manners: Managing Business Cultures in Europe. London: Nicholas Brealey

Moody, Bella / Gudykunst, William B. (eds.) (2002): Handbook of International and Intercultural Communication. London: Sage Publications

O´Hara-Deveraux, Mary / Johansen, Robert (1994): Global Work: Bridging Distance, Culture and Time. San Francisco, CA: Jossey-Bass

Ohmae, Kenichi (1990): The Borderless World. New York

Olsson, Micael (1985): Meeting Styles for Intercultural Groups AFS International: Occasional Papers in International Learning. No. 7, February 1985

Parker, Glenn M. (1994): Cross-Functional Collaboration. Training and Development (October 1994), 49–53

Parnell, M. / Vanderkloot, J. (1989): How to Build Cross-Cultural Bridges Communication World 8 (1989), 40–44

Rogers, Everett M. / Steinfatt, Thomas M. (1999): Intercultural Communication. Prospect Heights, IL: Waveland Press

Ruben, B. D. (1989): The Study of Cross-Cultural Competence: Traditions and Contemporary Issues. In: International Journal of Intercultural Relations 13 (1989), 229–240

Samovar, Larry A. / Porter, Richard E. (1999): Intercultural Communication: A Reader. 9th edition, Belmont, CA: Wadsworth

Sapir, Edward (1966): Culture, Language and Personality. Selected Essays Berkeley and Los Angeles, CA: University of California Press

Seelye, H. Ned / Seelye-James, Alan (1995): Culture Clash. Lincolnwood, IL: NTC Business Books

Storti, Craig (1989): The Art of Crossing Cultures. Yarmouth, ME: Intercultural Press

Tebould, J. C. Bruno / Chen, Ling / Fritz, Lynn M. (1994): Intercultural Organizational Communication Research in Multinational Organizations. In: International and Intercultural Annual 18 (1994), 12–29

Trompenaars, Fons (1993): Riding the Waves of Culture: Understanding Diversity in Global Business. London: Nicolas Brealey

Wiseman, Richard / Hammer, Mitchell R. / Nishida, Hiroko (1989): Predictors of Intercultural Communication Competence. In: International Journal of Intercultural Relations 13, No. 3 (1989), 349–362

Layout / Composition

Arnheim, Rudolf (1988): The Power of the Center: A Study of Composition in the Visual Arts. Berkeley, CA: University of California Press

Berger, John (1995): Ways of Seeing. New York: Viking Press

Clements, Ben (1974): Photographic Composition. Upper Saddle River, NJ: Prentice Hall

Grill, Tom / Scanlon, Mark (1990): Photographic Composition. New York: Amphoto

Lauer, David A. / Pentak, Stephen (1999): Design Basics. Belmont, CA: Wadsworth

Patterson, Freeman (1989): Photography and the Art of Seeing. Key Porter Books

Peterson, Bryan F. (1988): Learning to See Creatively. Toronto: Amphoto

Poore, Henry Rankin (1977): Composition in Art. New York: Dover Publications

Ward, Peter (1996): Picture Composition for Film and Television. Woburn, MA: Focal Press

Metaphors

Lakoff, George / Johnson, Mark (1980): Metaphors we live by. University of Chicago Press

Patton, P. (1993): Making Metaphors User Interface Design. In: ID 40, 2, 1993, 62–66

Smilowitz, Elisson, D.: Do Metaphors Make Web Browsers Easier to Use?
[http://www.baddesigns.com/mswebcnf.htm] (30.7.2000)

Methods

Beyer, H. / Holtzblatt, K. (1998): Contextual Design. Defining Customer-Centered Systems. San Francisco, CA: Morgan Kaufmann Publishers

Dayton, T. / McFarland, A. / Kramer, J. (1998): Bridging User Needs to Object Oriented GUI Prototypes via Task Object Design. In: Wood, L. (ed.): User Interface Design. Bridging the Gap from Requirements to Design. Boca Raton, FL: CRC Press, 15–56

Greenbaum, J. / Kyng, M. (1991): Design at Work. Cooperative Design of Computer Systems. Hillsdale, NJ: Lawrence Erlbaum Associates

Navigation

Donnelly, Vanessa (2000): Designing Easy-to-use Web Sites: A Hands-on Approach to Structuring Successful Websites. Reading, MA: Addison-Wesley

Fleming, Jennifer (1998): Web Navigation. Designing the User Experience. Beijing: O'Reilly

Gay, G. / Mazur, J. (1991): Navigating in hypermedia. In: Berk, E. & Devlin, J. (eds.): Hypertext/ hypermedia handbook. New York: McGraw-Hill

Reiss, Eric L. (2000): Practical Information Architecture: A Hands-On Approach to Structuring Successful Websites. Reading, MA: Addison-Wesley

Rivlin, E. / Botafogo, R. / Shneiderman, B. (1994): Navigating in hyperspace: Designing a structurebase toolbox. In: Communications of ACM, 37 (2), 1994, 87–96

Orientation

Arthur, Paul / Passini, Romedi (1992): Wayfinding. People, Signs, and Architecture. New York: McGraw-Hill

Downs, Roger M. / Stea, David (1977): Maps in Minds: Reflections on Cognitive Mapping. New York: HarperCollins

Florin, Fabrice (1990): Information Landscapes. In: Ambronn, Susann / Hooper, Kristina (eds.): Learning with Interactive Multimedia. Redmond: Cobb Group, 27–49

Irler, W. J. / Barbieri, G. (1993): Non-intrusive hypertext anchors and individual colour markings. In: Rizk, R. / Jonassen, David H.: Structural Knowledge. New Jersey: Hillsdale

Kahn, Paul / Lenk, Krsysztof (2001): Mapping Websites: Digital Media Design. Hove, UK: Rotovision

Lynch, Kevin (1960): The Image of the City. Cambridge, MA, London: MIT Press

Miller, George A. (1956): The Magic Number Seven, Plus or Minus Two: Some Limits on Our Capacity for Processing Information. In: Psychological Review, Vol. 63, No. 2, March 1956, 81–97

Nielsen, J. / Lyngbæk, U. (1990): Two field studies of hypermedia usability. In: McAleese, R. / Green, C. (eds.): Hypertext: State of the Art. Norwood, NJ: Ablex Publ., 64–72

Paivio, Allan (1986): Mental representations: A dual-coding approach. New York, Oxford

Simon, H. A. (1979): How Big is a Chunk? In: Models of Thought, New Haven: Yale University Press, 50–61

Personas

Braiterman, Jared (2002): Start now: Develop with users [http://www.macromedia.com/desdev/articles/user_design.html]

Cooper, Alan (1999): The Inmates Are Running The Asylum. Indianapolis, IN: SAMS

Cooper, Alan (2001): Goal-Directed® Design [http://www.cooper.com/articles/art_goal_directed_design.htm]

Cooper Interaction Design (2002): Concept Projects [http://www.cooper.com/concept_projects.htm]

Glaze, Geoff M. (1999): Personas for the S2S Project [http://www.cs.utexas.edu/users/almstrum/cs373/general/personas.html]

Goodwin, Kim (2001): Perfecting Your Personas [http://www.cooper.com/newsletters/2001_07/perfecting_your_personas.htm]

Pictures

Horn, Robert E. (1998): Visual Language. Global Communication for the 21st Century. Brainbridge Island, WA: MarcoVU

Horton, William (1991): Illustrating Computer Documentation. The Art of Presenting Information Graphically on Paper and Online. New York: John Wiley & Sons

Horton, William (1994b): Icon Book Visual Symbols for Computer Systems & Documentation. New York: John Wiley & Sons

Hutchinson, B. (1991): Using illustrations to improve communication: back to basics. In: British Journal of Educational Technology, 22 (1)

Komar, Vitaly / Melamid, Alexander (1999): Painting by Numbers. University of California Press

McCloud, Scott (1994): Understanding Comics The Invisible Art. North Amherst, MA: Kitchen Sink Press

Nöth, Winfried (ed.) (1997): Can Pictures Lie? In: Nöth, Winfried (ed.): Semiotics of the Media. State of the Art, Projects, and Perspectives. Berlin, New York: de Gruyter, 133–146

Tufte, Edward R. (2001): The Visual Display of Quantitative Information. 2nd edition, Cheshire, CT: Graphics Press

Ware, Colin (2000): Information Visualization. Perception for Design. San Francisco, CA: Morgan Kaufmann Publishers

Wildbur, Peter / Burke, Michael (1999): Information Graphics Innovative Solutions in Contemporary Design. London: Thames & Hudson

Project Management

England, Elaine / Finney, Andy (1999): Managing Multimedia. Harlow: Addison-Wesley

Rosenfeld, Louis / Morville, Peter (2002): Information Architecture for the World Wide Web. 2nd edition, Beijing: O'Reilly & Associates

Sano, Darrell (1996): Designing Large-Scale Web Sites A Visual Design Methodology. New York: John Wiley & Sons

Siegel, David (1997): Secrets of Successful Web Sites: Project Management on the World Wide Web. Indianapolis, IN: Hayden Books

Strauss, Roy (1997): Managing Multimedia Projects. Oxford: Focal Press

Zschau, O. / Traub, D. / Zahradka, R. (2002): Web Content Management. Websites professionell planen und gestalten. 2. Aufl., Bonn: Galileo

Reading

Dillon, A. (1992): Reading from Paper versus screens A critical review of the empirical literature. In: Ergonomics 3rd special issue on cognitive ergonomics 35 (10), 1297–1326

Gould, J. D. (1987): Reading slower from CRT displays than paper. Attempts to isolate a single-variable explanation. In: Human Factors, Vol. 29, No. 3

Wilkinson, R. T. / Robinshaw, H. M. (1987): Proof-reading. VDU and paper text compared for speed, accuracy and fatigue. In: Behavior and Information Technology, Vol. 6, No. 2, April–June 1987

Scrolling

Nielsen, Jakob (1996): Top Ten Mistakes in Web Design Alertbox May 1996 [http://www.useit.com/alertbox/9605.html]

Nielsen, Jakob (1997): Changes in Web Usability Since 1994. Alertbox 1.12.1997 [http://www.useit.com/alertbox/9712a.html]

Nielsen, Jakob (1999): »Top Ten Mistakes« Revisited Three Years Later Alertbox 2.5.1999 [http://www.useit.com/alertbox/990502.html]

Text Design

Dougherty, Dale (1997): Don´t Forget to Write. [http://www.webreview.com/1997/10_10/strategists/10_10_97_6.shtml]

Gould, J. D. / Alfaro, L. / Finn, R. / Haupt, B. / Minuto, A. / Salaun, J. (1987): Why reading was slower from CRT displays than from paper. In: Proc. ACM CHI+GI '87 (Toronto, Canada, 5.–9. April), 7–11

Gould, J. D. / Grischkowsky, N. (1984): Doing the same work with hard copy and with cathode ray tube (CRT) computer terminals. In: Human Factors 26, 323–337

Horn, Robert E. (1989): Mapping Hypertext. Analysis, Linkage, and Display of Knowledge for the Next Generation of On-Line Text and Graphics. Lexington, MA: Lexington Institute Press

Nielsen, Jakob (1996): Inverted Pyramids in Cyberspace. Alertbox June 1996. [http://www.useit.com/alertbox/9606.html]

Nielsen, Jakob (1997): How Users Read on the Web. Alertbox 1.10.1997. [http://www.useit.com/alertbox/9710a.html]

Nielsen, Jakob (1998): Writing for the Web. [http://www.sun.com/980713/webwriting]

Ohio State Research: Text on Computer Screens Harder to Understand, less Persuasive. [http:// www.acs.ohio-state.edu/units/research/archive/comptext.htm]

Wilkinson, R. T. / Robinshaw, H. M. (1987): Proof-reading: VDU and paper text compared for speed, accuracy and fatigue. In: Behaviour and Information Technology 6, 2 (April–June), 125–133

Wright, P. / Lickorish, A. (1983): Proof-reading texts on screen and paper. In: Behaviour and Information Technology 2, 3 (July–Sept.), 227–235

Typography

Adobe Type Library: [http://www.adobe.com/type]

Carson, David / Blackwell, Lewis (1995): The End of Print. San Francisco, CA: Chronicle Books

Cavanaugh, Sean (1997): Insiderbuch Type Design. Digitales Gestalten mit Schriften. Zürich: Midas

Spiekermann, Erik / Ginger, E. M. (1993): Stop Stealing Sheep & find out how type works. Mountain View, CA: Adobe Press

Walton, Roger (1997): Typographics 2 Cybertype. New York: Hearst Books

Williams, Robin / Davis, Nancy (1998): The Non-Designer's Type Book: Insights and Techniques for Creating Professional-Level Type. Berkeley, CA: Peachpit Press

Usability

Badre, Albert N. (2002): Shaping Web Usability: Interaction Design in Context. Reading, MA: Addison-Wesley

Brinck, Tom / Gergle, Darren / Wood, Scott D. (2001): Usability for the Web: Designing Web Sites that Work. San Francisco, CA: Morgan Kaufmann Publishers

Krug, S. (2000): Don´t make me think. A Common Sense Approach to Web Usability. Indianapolis, IN: New Riders Publishing

Nielsen, Jakob (1999): Designing Web Usability. Indianapolis, IN: New Riders Publishing

Pearrow, Marc (2000): Web Site Usability Handbook. Hingham, MA: Charles River Media

Spool, Jared M. / Scanlon, Tara / Schroeder, Will / Snyder, Carolyn / DeAngelo, Terri (1999): Web Site Usability. A Designer's Guide. San Francisco, CA: Morgan Kaufmann Publishers

Vora, P. R. / Helander, M. G. / Shalin, V. L. (1994): Evaluating the influence of interface styles and multiple access paths in hypertext. In: Proc. ACM CHI'94 Conf., 323–329

Video Language

Hochberg, J. / Brooks, V. (1978): The perception of motion pictures. In: Carterette, E. C. / Friedman, M. P. (eds.): Handbook of perception. Vol. X: Perceptual ecology. New York: Academic Press, 259–304

Marchese, F. T. (ed.) (1995): Understanding images Finding meanings in digital imagery. New York: Springer-Verlag

Mayer, R. E. / Anderson, R. B. (1992): The instructive animation: Helping students build connections between words and pictures in multimedia learning. In: Journal of Educational Psychology, 84, 444–452

Nielsen, Jakob (1997a): WebTV Usability Review. Alertbox 1. Febr. 1997 [http://www.useit.com/alterbox/9702a.html]

Nielsen, Jakob (1997b): TV Meets the Web. Alertbox 15. Febr. 1997 [http://www.useit.com/alertbox/9702b.html]

9.2 Style Guides and Other Sources on the Internet

Apple Computer, Inc. (1987): Apple Human Interface Guidelines The Apple Desktop Interface. Addison-Wesley

Apple Computer Inc.: *Human Interface Guidelines*
http://developer.apple.com/techpubs/macos8/HumanInterfaceToolbox/HumanInterfaceGuide/humaninterfaceguide.html

Association for Computing Machinery: *SIGCHI. Special Interest Group on Computer-Human Interaction*
http://www.acm.org/sigchi

Beck, Astrid: *gui Design*
http://www.gui-design.de

Berners-Lee, Tim, W3C: *Style Guide for Online Hypertext*
http://www.w3.org/Provider/Style/Overview.html

Cook, John: *The Sevloid Guide to Web Design*
http://www.sev.com.au/webzone/design.asp

Cooper, Alan: *Humanizing Technology*
http://www.cooper.com

Ergon Online. Informationsdienst Arbeit und Gesundheit, Schwerpunkt Bildschirmarbeit im Sozialnetz Hessen
http://www.sozialnetz-hessen.de/ergo-online/E_HOME.HTM

Flanders, Vincent: *Web Pages That Suck.Com*
http://www.webpagesthatsuck.com

Friedman, Steven Morgan: *Resources on Web Style*
http://www.westegg.com/unmaintained/badpages

IBM Corp.: *Ease of use*
http://www-3.ibm.com/ibm/easy/eou_ext.nsf/publish/561

IBM Corp.: *Web Guidelines*
http://www.ibm.com/ibm/hci/guidelines/web/print.html

International Journal of Human Computer Studies: *Special Issue – World Wide Web Usability*
http://ijhcs.open.ac.uk

Inxight: *Making Information Make Sense*
http://www.inxight.com

Isys Information Architects: *Interface Hall of Shame*
http://www.iarchitect.com/mshame.htm

Karp, Tony, TLC Systems Corp.: *Art and the Zen of web sites*
http://www.digiweb.com/tkarp/webtips.html

Lynch, Patrick J. / Horton, Sarah (2002): Web Style Guide: Basic Design Principles for Creating
  Web Sites. 2nd edition, Yale University Press

MacGregor, Chris: Flazoom.com
  http://www.flazoom.com

Microsoft Corp.: *Designing for the Web: Empirical Studies*
  http://www.microsoft.com/usability/webconf.htm

Nielsen, Jakob: *Alertbox*
  http://www.useit.com

SAP AG: *SAP Design Guild*
  http://www.sapdesignguild.org

Siegel, David: *Creating Killer Web Sites*
  http://www.killersites.com

Siegel, David: *Home Page*
  http://www.dsiegel.com

Society for Technical Communication
  http://www.stc.org

Sullivan, Terry: *All Things At Web*
  http://www.pantos.org/atw

SUN Microsystems: *SUN's New Web Design*
  http://www.sun.com/980113/sunonnet

Thissen, Frank: *Screen-Design*
  www.frank-thissen.de

Tognazzini, Bruce: *Home Page*
  http://www.asktog.com

Usable Web
  http://usableweb.com

User Interface Engineering
  http://world.std.com/~uieweb/

Webmonkey
  http://hotwired.lycos.com/webmonkey/design/?tw=design

Weinreich, Harald: *Software-Ergonomie und das World Wide Web*
  http://vsys-www.informatik.uni-hamburg.de/ergonomie/index.html

World Wide Web Consortium
  http://www.w3.org

Yale University: Yale Web Style Guide
  http://www.med.yale.edu/caim/manual/index.html

9.3 List of Illustrations and Sources

Page 16

Illustration: Wilhelm Busch. With the kind permission of the Wilhelm Busch Museum, Hannover, Georgengarten 1, 30167 Hannover, Germany

The illustrations at the beginning of the chapters are by the German painter Wilhelm Busch. Busch lived from 1832-1908 and was known for his illustrated stories, which are forerunners of the modern comics. In Germany, every child knows his most famous illustrated story Max and Moritz (1865).

Page 18

Quotation source: Gui Bonsiepe (1996): Interface. Design neu begreifen. Mannheim: Bollmann, 42

Photo: Frank Thissen

Page 20 + 21

Kiwilogic: http://www.kiwilogic.de/ kiwilogic/_xml/fs_index.php (Access: 08.07.2002)

Page 26

Illustration: Title page of the *Encyclopédie ou dictionnaire raisonné des sciences, des arts et des métiers, par une société de gens de lettres*, 1751

Page 27

The Atlantic Monthly: As We May Think http://www.theatlantic.com/unbound/ flashbks/computer/bushf.htm (Access 16.12.2002)

Page 28

Project Xanadu: http://xanadu.com

Page 30

Apple: Hypercard

Logo der ACM: http://www.acm.org

Page 31

W3C. World Wide Web Consortium: http://www.w3.org (Access: 28.03.2002)

Page 32

Nick Usborne (1998): It´s the Audience, Stupid!, In: Contentious, 17.11.1998 http://www.contentious.com/articles/1-8/ guest1-8b.html

Page 33

Cooper Interaction Design: http://www.cooper.com

I thank Cooper Interaction Design for the use of this illustration.

Page 34

Alan Cooper (1999): The Inmates Are Running The Asylum. Indianapolis: SAMS, S.126–127

Page 35

abc news: http://abc.abcnews.go.com

Page 36

Alan Cooper (1999): The Inmates Are Running The Asylum. Indianapolis: SAMS, S.124

Page 37

Alan Cooper (1999): The Inmates Are Running The Asylum. Indianapolis: SAMS, S.128

Page 38

Alan Cooper (1999): The Inmates Are Running The Asylum. Indianapolis: SAMS, S.124, 149, 151

Page 40

Photo: Frank Thissen

Page 41

Allianz: http://www.allianz.de

Stadtwerke Karlsruhe: http://www.stadtwerke-karlsruhe.de

AOL-Verlag: http://www.aol-verlag.de

Page 42

Microsoft: Encarta Enzyclopedia Standard 2001. 1993–2001

Spiegel: http://forum.spiegel.de/cgi-bin/ WebX?13@@.ee725eb

Page 43

Audi AG: http://www.audi.com/com/de/ home.jsp

Ebay: http://www.ebay.com

Page 44

blaxxun interactive: www.cybertown.com (15.7.2000)

Seminar Interkulturelle Kommunikation an der Hochschule der Medien Stuttgart

Page 45

Computer simulation of the imperial palace. Ingelheim, Germany. With the kind permission of ArchimediX. www.archimedix.de

Red Orb Entertainment: Riven. The Sequel to Myst. 1997

Page 48

Illustration: Wilhelm Busch. With the kind permission of the Wilhelm Busch Museum, Hannover, Georgengarten 1, 30167 Hannover, Germany

Page 50

Photo: Frank Thissen

Page 51

Lynch, Kevin: The Image of the City. The M. I. T. Press Massachusetts Institute of Technology, Cambridge, Massachusetts, and London, England 1960, 4

Photo: Frank Thissen

Page 52

Jacob Nielsen, U. Lyngbaek (1990): Two field studies of hypermedia usability. In: R. McAleese, C. Green (eds.): Hypertext: State of the Art, Ablex, 64–72

Jarred M. Spool et al. (1999): Web Site Usability. A Designer's Guide. San Francisco, CA: Morgan Kaufmann Publ., 15

Jarred M. Spool et al. (1999): Web Site Usability. A Designer's Guide. San Francisco, CA: Morgan Kaufmann Publ., 6

Page 54

LEGO GmbH: http://www.lego.com/deu/ legoland/deutschland/default.asp. LEGO is a registered trademark and is used here with the permission of the LEGO Group.

Page 55

Shiseido: http://www.shiseido.com.jp/ ELIXIR/html/index.htm

Nike: http://www.nike.com/usa/index.html

Page 56

Photo: Frank Thissen. With the kind permission of the Natural History Museum, Cromwell Road,London,SW7 5BD, United Kingdom

Page 57

LEGO Group: http://www.lego.com/ legolandnew/california/parkmap/ default.asp?locale=2057

LEGO is a registered trademark and is used here with the permission of the LEGO Group.

Page 58

DaimlerChrysler AG Stuttgart: A-Klasse. Die Zukunft des Automobils Version 2.0, Konzept und Realisation: SCHOLZ & VOLKMER, Wiesbaden 1998

Microsoft: Encarta Enzyclopedia Standard 2001. 1993–2001

Page 60

Kimura Karate: http://www.kimura-karate.ch

Page 61

Kimura Karate: http://www.kimura-karate.ch

DaimlerChrysler AG Stuttgart: Die neue E-Klasse. 1995

Page 62

Adobe Systems Incorporated: Tutorial zu Photoshop 4.0

Ravensburger AG, Burda GmbH: Bitte nicht stören! 1995

Page 63

Siemens AG: http://www.my-siemens.com

Schweppes: http://www.schweppes.de/ htm/set.htmset.htm (15.12.2002)

SAP AG: http://www.sap.de

Lingubot: http://www.elbot.com/

At the races: http://www.attheraces.co.uk/ ukro/html/detection.html?interactionMana ger=attheraces

For more information on the advisors, see
http://www.kiwilogic.de

Page 64
Taurus Video: Laurel & Hardy. Hal Roach
Studio Tour. 1996

Page 65
Medialab: W.&L.T. Interactive 2. 1996

Stadtverwaltung St.Gallen: http://
www.stgallen-i.ch/indexd.htm (19.2.1999)

Page 66
HEUREKA-Klett Softwareverlag,
Stuttgart: Opera fatal. 1996. Production:
Ruske&Puehretmaier, Wiesbaden

Page 67
KinderCampus AG: http://
www.kindercampus.de (15.9.2000)

Page 68
Dorlington Kindersley: My First Incredible,
Amazing Dictionary. 1995

Page 69
MGM Media Gruppe München: Bewegte
Werbung. Die Geschichte des deutschen
Werbefilms. 1996

Page 70–71
Amnesty International USA: Amnesty
Interactive. 1994, 1995

Page 72
Apple: http://www.apple.com

Yahoo!: http://dir.yahoo.com/Arts/Visual_
Arts/Calligraphy/Artists

Page 73
Bauhaus-Archiv. Designmuseum:
http://www.bauhaus.de

Page 74 & 75
Photo: Carolyn Gale, Stanford University

Page 76
SAP AG: http://www.sap.com (Januar
1997)

SAP AG: http://www.sap.com (12.7.2002)

Page 77
Yahoo!: http://www.yahoo.com

Ebay: http://wwwebay.com

Amazon: http://www.amazon.com

Page 78
Brandt: http://www.brandt-zwieback.de/
english/portrait/set.htm

Spektrum Verlag: Evolution. 1995

Page 79
Microsoft: Encarta Enzyclopedia Standard
2001. 1993–2001

eLibrary: Encyclopedia.com
http://www.encyclopedia.com/html/w/
ww1w1eb.asp

Apple: http://www.apple.com/powerbook/

Page 80
Microsoft: Encarta Enzyclopedia Standard
2001. 1993–2001

Artemide: http://www.artemide.com/eng/
index.html

Tivola Verlag GmbH & Co KG: Max und
die Geheimformel. 1995

Page 81
Amazon: http://www.amazon.com

Business Week Online:
http://www.businessweek.com

Page 82
Wrangler: http://www.wrangler.com/
pages/sitemap.asp?sid=2032869291

Opera Theatre St. Louis: http:
//www.opera-stl.org/SiteOne/flash/
index.html

Page 83
DaimlerChrysler AG Stuttgart:
www.mercedes-benz.com/d/menu/
search/s_map_frame.htm?_back=
www.mercedes-benz.com/d/default.htm
(21.6.2000)

Yakult: http://www.yakult.co.jp/products/
index.html

Page 84
Inxight Software: http://www.inxight.com/
products/vizserver/demos.php

Page 85
Google: http://www.google.com/
advanced_search?hl=en

House of Parliament: http://
www.parliament.uk/index/index2.cfm

Page 90
Illustration: Wilhelm Busch. With the kind permission of the Wilhelm Busch Museum, Hannover, Georgengarten 1, 30167 Hannover, Germany

Page 94
Quotation source: David Siegel [http://www.writing.uct.ac.za/visual/typograp.htm]

Microsoft: http://www.microsoft.com Permanently set font in the browser: Arabia.

Page 98
Apollinaris: http://www.apollinaris.de/espanol/index.html

Ilford: http://www.ilford.com/html/us_english/bw.html

Page 99
Yakult: www.yakult.co.jp/english/company/food_2/index.htm

Aral: http://www.aral.pl/iof/inf_o_f.htm

Page 100
Joshua Davis: Praystation http://www.praystation.com

Weworkforthem: http://www.weworkforthem.com

Alins Ilstración: http://www.alinsilustracion.com

Sony Ericsson: http://www.sonyericssonmobile.com/in/spg.jsp?page=start

Page 102
Jakob Nielsen: Alertbox http://www.useit.com/alertbox/9710a.htm

Page 104
Adobe: http://www.adobe.com/products/photoshopel/main.html

Shiseido: http://www.shiseido.co.jp/e/story/htlm/st30700.htm

Page 105
Nestle AG: http://www.nesvita.com.ph/why-you-need.htm

Adobe: http://www.adobe.com/products/acrobat/main.html

Page 106
Financial Times Deutschland: http://news.ft.com/home/rw/

CNN: http://www.cnn.com/2002/WORLD/europe/10/28/moscow.gas/index.html

Page 107
Renault AG: http://www.renault.com/gb/produits/espace.htm

Jakob Nielsen: Alertbox http://www.useit.com/alertbox/20020722.htm

Page 108
Adobe: http://www.adobe.com

Eizo: http://www.eizo.com/products/index.html

Page 109
Opera Theatre of Saint Louis: http://www.opera-stl.org/SiteOne/flash/index.html

Page 110
Renault: http://www.renault.com/gb/produits/coupe2.htm

Microsoft: Encarta Enzyclopedia Standard 2001. 1993–2001

Page 111
Miami.com: http://www.miami.com/mld/miami/

Page 112
Miami.com: http://www.miami.com/mld/miami/living/education/3742731.htm

Page 113
Apple: http://www.apple.com/macosx

MGM Media Gruppe München: Bewegte Werbung. Die Geschichte des deutschen Werbefilms. 1996

Page 114
Daimler-Chysler AG: http://www.usa.mercedesbenz.com

Page 115
Osbourne: http://www.osborne.es

Page 116–117
Microsoft: Encarta Enzyclopedia Standard 2001. 1993–2001

Page 118
Bob Dylan. Highway 61 Interactive. 1995

Appendix

Weinkellerei Meraner:
http://www.meraner.at

Page 119
Antwerpes & Partner AG: »In Bytes We
Trust«. 1996

The Body Shop: http://www.the-body-
shop.com

Saab: http://www.saab.com

Page 120
Nestle: http://www.alete.de/detect_
flash.htm

New Zealand Wool Group: http://
www.woolgroup.co.nz/about/index.html

Coca Cola: http://www.cocacola.jp/
products/cocacola/index.html

Fiat: http://www.fiat.co.uk

Menschen für Tierrechte Bayern e.V.:
http://www.animal2000.org

Page 121
USM Möbelbausysteme, U. Schärer Söhne
AG, Schweiz 1998, Realisierung: Scholz &
Volkmer, Wiesbaden

United Soft Media Verlag GmbH: Route
66. München. 1996

Tivola Verlag GmbH: Wellen, Wracks und
Wassermänner. 1996

Hewlett Packard: *Looney Colors. Ein
interaktiver Spielfilm von Hewlett Packard.*
1997

Page 124
Horton, William (1994): The Icon Book.
Visual Symbols for Computer Systems and
Documentation. New York: John Wiley &
Sons, 16

Page 126
Functionality of icons: Get Mails, Send
Mails, Get/Send Mails, Get All Mails, Send
All Mails, Get/Send All Mails
[http://www.akmail.com]

Page 128
Susan Kare: MacIntosh Icons (Web Site:
http://www.kare.com)

Page 130
BKK Bundesverband: Yellow Silver. 1996

Page 131
U. Schärer Söhne AG, Schweiz: USM
Möbelbausysteme 1998, Realisierung:
Scholz & Volkmer, Wiesbaden

Microsoft AG: Encarta Enzyclopedia
Standard 2001. 1993–2001

Page 132
Microsoft AG: Encarta Enzyclopedia
Standard 2001. 1993–2001

Page 133
Quotation Source: Spool, Jared M. / et al.
(1999): Web Site Usability. A Designer's
Guide. San Francisco, CA: Morgan
Kaufmann Publ., 89

Page 134
Quotation Source: http://
www.macromedia.com/software/flash/
productinfo/usability/tips

Page 135
Jaguar: http://www.x-type.com

Nazario Foto: http://www.nazariofoto.it/
ita/index.html

VMMa—JIMtv: http://jim.be/tv/programs

Page 136
Timbuk2: http://www.timbuk2.com

Okty: http://www.okty.com

Page 137
Sony: http://www.sonyclassical.com/
music/ 89469/main.html

Page 142
Illustration: Wilhelm Busch. With the
kind permission of the Wilhelm Busch
Museum, Hannover, Georgengarten 1,
30167 Hannover, Germany

Page 144
Shiseido: http://www.sca.shiseido.com/
main.cfm?select= home&flash=yes

Page 145
Audi AG: http://www.audiusa.com/family/
home/0,,familyId-4,00.html

Page 146–147
I thank my colleague Konrad Baumann
from the Technical College Joanneum Graz
(http://www.fh-joanneum.at) for creating
and providing the illustrations.

The Eyegaze System of the LC technologies Company was used. The system functions purely visually with an infrared diode, camera, graphics card, and software from LC Technologies (http://www.eyegaze.com).

Page 148
Microsoft: Encarta Enzyklopädie Professional 2003. 1993–2002

Amnesty International USA: Amnesty Interactive. 1994, 1995

Page 149
Cosmopolitan: http://www.cosmopolitan.com

Brandt: http://www.brandt-zwieback.de/english/portrait/set.htm

Volvo: http://www.volvocars.co.i/Content/V70/V70.asp

Page 150
Medialab: W.&.L.T. Interactive 2. 1996

DaimlerChrysler AG Stuttgart: Die neue E-Klasse. 1995

Page 151
Coca Cola: http://www.cocacola.fr/historique/historique.htm

E.M.M.E. Interactive: Der Louvre. 1995

Page 152
Google: http://www.google.com

Page 153
Amazon: http://www.amazon.com

Kiwilogic: http://www.kiwilogic.de/kiwilogic/_xml/fs_index.php?sprache=us

Page 154
Apollinaris: http://www.apollinaris.de/esoanol/index.html

Page 155
Deutsche Lufthansa AG: http://www.be-lufthansa.com/jobs_and_career.html

Page 156
Lavazza: http://www.lavazza.com/com/jsp/web/templates/navigazione/navigatore_COM.jsp?idNode=151

Nestle: http://www.nestle.co.uk/recipes/desserts

Page 157
Hush Puppies: http://www.hush-puppies.com

Page 158
Te Puni Koriki. Ministry of Maori Development: http://www.tpk.govt.nz

Die Zeit: http://www.zeit.de

Medialab: W.&.L.T. Interactive 2. 1996

Apple: http://www.apple.com

Page 159
Amnesty International USA: Amnesty Interactive. 1994, 1995

Page 161
Erikotten Artwork: http://www.erikotten.muizenpraat.nl/website/links.php

Deutsche Lufthansa AG: http://www.be-lufthansa.com/jobs_and_career.html

Eizo: http://www.eizo.de/r2001/index_ie.htm

Page 165
The Body Shop: http://www.the-body-shop.com

Antwerpes AG: http://www.antwerpes.de/english/index.htm

Breitling: http://www.breitling.com/eng/models/windrider/index.html

Page 166
Medialab: W.&.L.T. Interactive 2. 1996

Milla & Partner: http://www.milla.de

Mitsubishi Motors: http://www.i-move-u.com

X Nographics: http://www.xnographics.com

Page 167
Wilhelma Stuttgart: http://www.wilhelma.de/de

Page 170
Het Muziektheater: http://www.het-muziektheater.com/index2.htm

Alins Ilustración: http://www.alinsilustration.com

Page 171
Kimuar Karate: http://www.kimura-karate.ch

Fancyphone: http://www.fancyphone.es/eng/home_i.htm

Page 174

Antwerpes AG: http://www.antwerpes.de/english/index.htm

Coca Cola: http://www.fanta.de

Page 175

Sixt: http://www.e-sixt.de

Dsemotion: http://www.dsemotion.com/site/home.asp

Page 178

Moon Music: http://www.moon-music.ch

Shell: http://www2.shell.com/home/Framework

Page 179

Kodak: http://www.kodak.gr/GR/el/nav/news.shtml

Shell AG: http://www.shell-direct-partner.de

Page 182

Sony Ericsson: http://www.sonyericssonmobile.com/spg.jsp?page=start&ver=portalpage_flash

Alere: http://www.alere.it/home.html

Page 183

Logan: http://www.hellologan.com

Ellumination Net: http://www.e-llumination.net

Page 186

Braun: http://www.braun.com/braun/global/products/shavinggrooming.html

Beiersdorf AG: http://www.nivea.com/frameset.php

Page 187

IBM: http://www.ibm.com

Apollinaris: http://www.apollinaris.de/espanol/index.html

Page 190

Whizzart: http://www.whizzart.nl/nl/main.shtml

Celine Clanet: http://perso.club-internet.fr/fauveaux/celinette

Page 191

CroWeb Design: http://www.croweb.nl/crowizz.html

ArtTattoo: http://www.arttattoo.ch/html/index.htlm

Page 194

Flavored Thunder Media: http://www.flavoredthunder.com/index9-2000.shtml

Humanface:http://www.humanface.com/www

Page 195

Qdodge: http://www.qdodge.com/index_outofservice.asp

Adamdom: http://www.adamdom.com

Page 198

Mamalion: http://www.mamalion.com/about.html

Renée Rhyner: http://www.reneerhyner.com/index_IE.htm

Page 199

Marbert: http://www.marbert.de

New Image Creative Web Solution GmbH: http://www.terminmaschine.de

Page 202

Nikon: http://www.nikon.de/index_new.php3

Afri Cola: http://www.afri-cola.de

Page 203

Hasselblad: http://www.hasselblad.com

Bauhaus Archiv: http://www.bauhaus.de/english/index.htm

Page 206

Brooklyn Digital Foundry: http://www.brooklynfoundry.com

Conclave Obscurum: http://cmart.design.ru

Page 207

DaimlerChrysler AG: http://www.mercedes-benz.com/index_ie.htm

Greyscale: http://www.greyscale.net/LO1/index.html

Page 210
Shiseido: http://www.shiseido.de/shiseido/ home/products?Line=58&LineName=D% FCfte

Blue & Yellow Creative: http://www.blue-yellow.com/mo

Page 211
Bill Hicks: http://www.billhicks.com/main

Arremide: http://www.artemide.com/eng/ index.html

Page 214
Illustration: Wilhelm Busch. With the kind permission of the Wilhelm Busch Museum, Hannover, Georgengarten 1, 30167 Hannover, Germany

Page 217
10eG Visual: Schwerelos Das Tauchkompendium. 1998

Page 218
Systhema Verlag GmbH: Rocklexikon. 1999

Page 219
Antwerpes & Partner AG: »In Bytes We Trust«. 1996

Page 220
Amazon: https://www.amazon.com

Page 221
U. Schärer Söhne AG, Schweiz: USM Möbelbausysteme. 1998, Realization: Scholz & Volkmer, Wiesbaden

Page 223
Antwerpes AG: http://www.antwerpes.de/ english/index.htm

ABC News: http://abc.abcnews.go.com/ daytime/dt_home.html

Page 226
Illustration: Wilhelm Busch. With the kind permission of the Wilhelm Busch Museum, Hannover, Georgengarten 1, 30167 Hannover, Germany

Page 231
Loronix: Bad Day http://www.loronix.com/ products/video_clips/index.asp

Page 232
Illustration from: Schulz von Thun, Friedemann (1981): Miteinander reden. Störungen und Klärungen. Reinbek: Rowohlt, 25

Page 233
Faber Castell: http://www.faber-castell.de

Page 234
Hugo Boss: http://www.hugoboss.com/ deutsch/indexf.html#

Pepsi: http://www.pepsi.com (24.9.1998)

Nikon: http://www.nikon.com

Burger King: http://www.burgerking.com

Page 235
Fort Worth Opera: http://www.fwopera.org

AXA: http://www.axa.com/default1.asp

Yahoo!: http://www.yahoo.com

Page 236
Baskinrobbins: http://www.baskinrobbins.com/treats/

Page 237
Pizza Hut: http://www.pizzahut.com/ more.asp

Golf Online GmbH: http://www.golf.de/ langer/frameload.cfm?subsite=langer&sub site=home

Breitling: http://www.breitling.com/eng/ index_navitimer50.html

Page 238
Nexus Group GmbH: All about Eve http://www.talbotrunhof.com

Stadtwerke Karlsruhe GmbH: www.karlsruhe.de/Stadtwerke (4.9.1997)

Wolford: http://www.wolford.com/htm_d/ Welcome.htm

Page 239
Jesus Freaks Hamburg: http:// www.jesusfreaks.com (22.3.1999)

Lomo-Botschaft Baden-Württemberg: http://www.disinfo.de/lomo (21.2.1999)

Page 241
Jaguar: http://www.www.us.jaguar.com

Page 242
Lynx Viewer: http://www.delorie.com/web/lynxview.html

Page 243
Microsoft: Download Center http://www.microsoft.com/downloads/release.asp?releaseid=42706&area=top&ordinal=3
Jacob Nielsen: http://www.useit.com/alertbox/subscribe.html
Adobe: http://www.adobe.com

Page 244
Verena Osgyan, Andrea Lacusteanu und Christian Buchner: Cosi fan tutte—an interactive CD-ROM with a brutally beautiful puppet theater version of the opera, a spectacular karaoke function, and a lot of useless but highly interesting information about Wolfgang Amadeus Mozart.

Page 245
Joe Boxer: http://www.joeboxer.com/Joeboxer/poodle/poodle_smoke.html (5.5.1998)
Monty Python: dailyllama.com/news/index.html

Page 248
Illustration: Wilhelm Busch. With the kind permission of the Wilhelm Busch Museum, Hannover, Georgengarten 1, 30167 Hannover, Germany

Page 250
Quote: R.W. Brislin: Cross-cultural encounters. New York/Frankfurt 1981, 3
Nestle: http://www.nestle.co.kr

Page 251
Quote: Lewis, Richard D. (1999): When Cultures Collide. London: Nicholas Brealey Publ., 33

Page 252
Nestle: http://www.nestle.es

Page 253
Maletzke, Gerhard (1996): Interkulturelle Kommunikation. Opladen: Westdeutscher Verlag, 48

Page 254
Illustration according to Geert Hofstede (2001): Lokales Denken, globales Handeln. München: dtv, 9

Page 255
Japanese Kimono: http://www.japanesekimono.com

Page 256
White House: http://www.whitehouse.gov
Kodak: http://www.kodak.co.th
Kodak: http://www.kodak.be/BE/nl/corp/indexNE.shtml

Page 257
Wools of New Zealand: http://www.fernmark.com/about/standard_au.asp
Kodak: http://www.gr/GR/el/nav/takingPictures.shtml
Kodak: http://www.kodak.nl

Page 258–259
Yakult: http://www.yakult.co.jp

Page 260
Quotation Source: Lewis, Richard, D. (1996): When Cultures Collide. London: Nicholas Brealay Publ., 36

Page 261
Quotation Source: Lewis, Richard, D. (1996): When Cultures Collide. London: Nicholas Brealay Publ., 41

Page 262
Ministery of Education Finland: http://www.minedu.fi

Page 263
Jamaica Travel: http://www.jamaicatravel.com
Deutscher Bundestag: http://www.bundestag.de/htdocs_e/index.html

Page 264
Nestle: http://www.nestle.com

Page 265
Nestle: http://www.nestle.co.za

Page 266–267
Nestle: http://www.nestle.com.au

Page 268–269
Nestle: http://www.nestle.de

Page 270
Nestle: http://www.nestle.ru

Page 271
Nestle: http://www.nestlecaribbean.com

Page 272
Nestle: http://www.nestle.ph

Page 273
Nestle: http://www.nestle.it

Page 276
Illustration: Wilhelm Busch. With the
kind permission of the Wilhelm Busch
Museum, Hannover, Georgengarten 1,
30167 Hannover, Germany

Page 279
The illustration of the braille line BRAILLEX
ELBA2 is used with the permission of F.H.
Papenmeier GmbH & Co. KG, Schwerte,
Germany (http://www.papenmeier.de).

CNN: http://www.cnn.com

Page 280
Alessi: http://www.alessi.com/flash.htm

Romandson: http://www.romandson.com

Page 281
Tim Berners-Lee:
http://www.anybrowser.org/campaign/

Franz-Joseph Hanke: http://
www.einfach-fuer-alle.de/ navlink_s03_
4427.html?printversion=0

Jens Bertrams: http://www.einfach-
fuer-alle.de/ navlink_s03_
4427.html?printversion=0

Page 282
Apple: http://www.apple.com

Microsoft: http://www.microsoft.com/
ms.htm

Page 284
W3C: Web Accessibility Initiative
http://www.w3.org/WAI

Page 285
University Wisconsin-Madison: Designing a
More Usable World—for all
http://trace.wisc.edu/world

Page 288
W3C: HTML Validator Service
http://validator.w3.org

University Toronto: Bobby Worldwide
http://dev.cast.org/bobby3.2

Page 289
University of Philadelphia: WAVE 2.01
http://www.temple.edu/inst_disabilities/
piat/wave

Anybrowser: http://www.anybrowser.org

Page 290
Stanford University: Vischeck
http://www.vischeck.com

Lynx Viewer: http://www.delorie.com/web/
lynxview.html

Page 291
Fraunhofer Institut FIT. Institut angewandte
Informationstechnik: http://
www.fit.fraunhofer.de/projekte/iris/index.x
ml?aspect=Nutzerstudie

Page 300
Illustration: Wilhelm Busch. With the
kind permission of the Wilhelm Busch
Museum, Hannover, Georgengarten 1,
30167 Hannover, Germany

9.4 Index

Topic 54
Types of Reaction 218
Typography 94

U

Understandable Text 109
User-Oriented Design 32
Use of Color 164
US Federal Government 284

V

Validation Service 288
Values 254
Verdana 96
Video 130
Virtual Communities 44
Vischeck 290
Vision Registration Camera 147
Visual Disabilities 278
Visual Elements 70
Visual Structure 108

W

WAVE 289
Weizenbaum, Joseph 228
White 208
Wizards 61
World Wide Web 31
World Wide Web Consortium (W3C) 284

X

Xanadu 28

Y

Yellow 176

9.5 About the Author

Prof. Dr. Frank Thissen teaches the subjects Multimedia Communication, Multimedia Didactics, and Information Design at the College of Media, Stuttgart, Germany, and at the University of Karlsruhe, Germany. Previously he worked in industry where he was responsible for projects in Technical Documentation, Training and Continuing Education with electronic media and Internet/ Intranet.

His research activities focus on multimedia didactics; new forms of virtual, dialog-oriented learning; screen design; and the evaluation of Internetbased learning and informational material.

Frank Thissen is involved with LearnTec (European Conference for Educational Technology and Employee Training. www.learntec.de) and a member of various expert committees in the area of lifelong learning with new media.

You can find further information under:
www.frank-thissen.de

Contact:
frank@frank-thissen.de